Mastering the Sous Vide Technique: Essential Tips and Tricks

Ava J. Nelson

All rights reserved. Copyright © 2023 Ava J. Nelson

Funny helpful tips:

Practice regular physical activity; it boosts health and mood.

Limit the intake of fried foods; they can be high in unhealthy fats and calories.

Mastering the Sous Vide Technique: Essential Tips and Tricks : Unlock the Secret to Perfectly Cooked Gourmet Meals with Expert Sous Vide Techniques

Life advices:

Celebrate differences; they add richness to the relationship.

In the ocean of opportunities, dive deep, explore the unknown, and treasure the gems you find.

Introduction

This is a comprehensive culinary handbook that introduces readers to the fascinating world of sous vide cooking. This innovative cooking technique has been gaining popularity in recent years, and this guide aims to demystify the process, providing both beginners and experienced cooks with the knowledge and skills to achieve restaurant-quality results in the comfort of their own kitchens.

The book begins by delving into the fundamentals of sous vide, answering questions about what it is and how it works. It dispels the notion that sous vide is merely boiling food in a bag and explores the rich history of this cooking method. The benefits of sous vide are highlighted, emphasizing how it produces perfectly cooked, tender, and flavorful dishes, particularly meat and proteins.

To embark on a sous vide journey, readers are introduced to the necessary equipment. From sous vide machines, water ovens, and immersion circulators to DIY setups using simple household items like a cooler, kettle, and thermometer, the guide covers a range of options to suit different budgets and needs. Additionally, it explains the importance of vacuum sealers and food-safe bags in preserving the integrity and safety of the food during the cooking process.

With a detailed overview of the setup process, the book guides readers step-by-step in getting started with sous vide. It emphasizes food safety measures, ensuring that readers understand the importance of using food-safe bags and maintaining proper cooking temperatures for various ingredients.

As readers become more familiar with the sous vide technique, the guide offers advanced techniques and innovative methods. It explores creative approaches, such as using handheld smokers, soda siphons, and molecular gastronomy chemicals to elevate culinary creations. Additionally, the book explores ways to simplify cooking with sous vide, including reheating previously cooked food and incorporating sous vide with other cooking techniques.

The heart of this book lies in its vast collection of delicious recipes, spanning various categories from breakfast to desserts. Each section provides detailed instructions on how to cook specific ingredients to perfection, including chicken, beef, pork, seafood, vegetables, and more. The book also introduces readers to the art of making pickles, relishes, and chutneys, expanding the culinary possibilities with sous vide.

Throughout the guide, safety and proper cooking methods are emphasized, ensuring that readers can confidently experiment with new recipes and techniques. It encourages readers to convert their favorite traditional recipes into sous vide versions, unlocking the full potential of this innovative cooking method.

In conclusion, this is an invaluable resource for anyone intrigued by this new culinary trend. With a wealth of knowledge, practical tips, and a diverse range of delectable recipes, this guide equips readers with the skills to master the art of sous vide cooking and elevate their culinary adventures to a whole new level.

Contents

Understanding This New Culinary Trend 1
The Necessary Equipment 12
Getting Started 48
Advanced Techniques 70
Breakfast 81
    The Perfect Egg 82
    Sweet Potato and Pork Belly Hash 83
    Hollandaise Sauce 85
    Eggs Benedict 86
    Eggs Florentine 87
    Scrambled Eggs 88
    Asparagus and Prosciutto Scrambled Eggs 90
    Breakfast Burrito 92
    Overnight Oatmeal 94
    Applesauce 95
Appetizers 96
    Buffalo Chicken Wings 97
    Honey Garlic Chicken Wings 99
    Hummus 102
    Baba Ghanouj 104
    White Bean and Artichoke Dip 105
    Shrimp and Avocado Salsa 107
    Tomato and Mango Salsa 109
    Shrimp and Jalapeño Quesadilla 110

Deep-Fried Pork Belly Skewers with Honey Garlic Glaze 113
Tomato Confit and Provolone Grilled Cheese Sandwich Wedges 115
Flank Steak, Apricot, and Brie Bites..117
Pork Tenderloin, Tomato, and Bocconcini Canapés 119

Soups and Salads..122
Potato and Green Bean Salad with Honey Lemon Vinaigrette...........................123
Bacon and Egg Potato Salad 125
Bean Salad..127
Flank Steak, Mandarin Orange, and Spinach Salad 129
Chicken and Caesar Salad..131
Duck Breast and Arugula Salad with Blueberry Vinaigrette 133
Blueberry Vinaigrette..135
Spicy Butternut Squash Soup 137
Pumpkin and Apple Soup 139
Pork Belly and Udon Noodle Soup...141
Dashi Stock 145

Chicken 146
The Ultimate Chicken Breast..147
Rosemary Chicken with Cognac Mushroom Cream Sauce 149
Chicken with Tomato Pineapple Chutney 152
Chicken with Bruschetta and Basil 154
Indian Butter Chicken 156
Ancho Chicken Fajitas 158
Buffalo Chicken Naan Pizza 160
Chicken and Pepperoni Pizza Wraps...162
Chicken Shawarmas 164
Chicken Cacciatore 166

Barbecue Chicken on a Bun..168
Crispy Hoisin-Glazed Chicken Drumsticks..170
Crispy Barbecue Chicken Drumsticks...173
Crispy Sous Vide Chicken Wings..175

Beef...176
The Perfect Steak..177
Steak with Herb Compound Butter...179
Steak and Scallops with Chipotle Cream..182
Steak with Serrano Chili Chimichurri..185
Steak with Tropical Salsa..187
Steak with Bourbon Mushroom Sauce..189
Flank Steak Banh Mi Sandwiches with Sriracha Lime Mayo................................191
Coffee and Chocolate Flank Steak Tacos...193
Double-Seared Beef Tenderloin..195
Beef Tenderloin Medallions on Creamed Spinach and Potato Mash....................197
Beef Tenderloin Medallions with Red Wine and Portobello Mushroom Sauce......199
Beer-Braised Beef and Swiss Melt..201
Beef Goulash...203
Short Ribs with Pearl Onions and Balsamic Reduction..205
Deconstructed Cuban Boliche...207

Pork..210
Korean Pork Ribs...211
Barbecue Pork Ribs...214
Honey Garlic Pork Ribs...216
Orange Hoisin Pork Chops..218
Thai Pork Chops with Green Curry Sauce..220
24-Hour Sous Vide Pork Belly...223

Curried Pork Tenderloin with Mint Yogurt Sauce 225

Herb and Garlic Pork Tenderloin with Rose Sauce and Gnocchi 227

Pork Carnitas with Pico de Gallo 229

Barbecue Pulled Pork 231

Pulled Pork Shepherd's Pie 233

Asian Pork Lettuce Wraps 235

Seafood 237

Korean Shrimp 238

Garlic Butter Shrimp 240

Pasta with Shrimp and Roasted Red Pepper Cream Sauce 242

Shrimp Creole 244

Salmon with Edamame and Corn Succotash 246

Salmon with Orange Butter Sauce and Pickled Fennel 248

Salmon with Sun-Dried Tomato Basil Compound Butter 250

No-Fuss Scallops 252

Jerk Fish Tacos with Pineapple Coconut Salsa 254

Mahi-Mahi with Blush Sauce and Pasta 256

Mahi-Mahi with Peach and Mango Chutney 258

Halibut with Sicilian Ragu 259

Other Meats 261

Holiday Turkey Breast 262

Turkey Breast with Pistachio Mushroom Dressing 264

Turkey Breast with Apple Cranberry Chutney 266

Succulent Duck Breast 268

Duck Breast with Basil Pesto and Pomegranate Reduction 269

Herb-Infused Lamb Chops 272

Lamb Chops with Lemon Mint and Black Olive Butter 274

- Lamb Chops with Roasted Grapes and Feta 276
- Rack of Lamb with Caper Cream Sauce 278
- Moroccan Rack of Lamb with Mint Garlic Yogurt Sauce 280
- Venison Steak with Chipotle Lime Compound Butter 282
- Oxtails on Roasted Garlic Potato Mash 284
- Alligator Po-Boy Sandwiches with Cajun Mayo 286

Vegetables and Other Sides 288
- Green Bean Almandine 289
- Honey Ginger Carrots 291
- Mashed Potatoes 292
- Maple Butternut Squash Purée 294
- Leek and Cauliflower Purée 295
- Szechuan Broccoli 296
- Buttered Corn on the Cob 298
- Ratatouille 299
- Chickpea and Carrot Moroccan Stew 301
- Wild Mushroom and Leek Risotto 303
- Risotto with Parmesan and Peas 305

Desserts 307
- Apple Crisp 308
- Dulce de Leche 310
- Spiced Pumpkin Purée 311
- Peaches with Brandy 314
- Strawberries and Grand Marnier 316
- Crème Anglaise 317
- Pears with Port 318
- Mango Pistachio Rice Pudding 320

Rum Raisin and Pecan Rice Pudding 322
Eggnog 324
Pickles, Relishes, and Chutneys 326
    Pickled Dilly Beans 327
    Bread and Butter Pickles 329
    Garlic Dill Pickle Spears 331
    Spicy Pickled Fennel 333
    Vietnamese Pickled Carrots and Daikon 335
    Pickled Red Onions 337
    Pickled Jalapeño Escabeche 339
    Pickled Turnips 341
    Zucchini Relish 343
    Sweet Cucumber Relish 345
    Tomato Pineapple Chutney 347
    Peach and Mango Chutney 349

Chapter 1
Understanding This New Culinary Trend

Innovation is something that people generally love. Whether it is a new feature in a smartphone, gel in the soles of shoes, or some new way to play a video game, development of new ideas and technology is always popular. The kitchen is not immune to innovation—quite the contrary in fact. There always seems to be some new gadget, appliance, or tool developed to make cooking easier. Recently, a new culinary trend has been gaining steam in the home kitchen. Sous vide, which has been used in restaurants and commercial kitchens since the 1970s, has started to see significant growth in the home kitchen market. With the development of sous vide kitchen appliances specifically designed for the home cook, this new way to cook is really growing in popularity.

What Is Sous Vide?

The term *sous vide* is French and the direct translation is "under vacuum." This method cooks food that has been placed in a food-safe bag and vacuum sealed. Once the food is sealed in the bag and all the air removed, it is then placed in a temperature-controlled water bath. Since water is a much better conductor of energy than air, the water that surrounds the bag, and comes right up against the food, heats all that is in the bag in an efficient and effective way. Once the bag has been in the water for the allotted time, the food is removed from the bag and often ready to be served. It is that easy.

FACT

Sous and *vide* are both French words, with *sous* meaning "under" and *vide* meaning "vacuum." Together these words describe the technique that is used in sous vide cooking, where meat or other food is vacuum sealed in a food-safe bag, dropped in a hot-water bath, and then cooked.

How Does It Work?

The basic premise of most cooking, whether using an oven, stovetop, or grill, is that the heat is generally much higher than the target internal temperature of the meat. Consider cooking a steak on the grill. The grill is fired up and the lid is closed to get that grill very hot. Usually grills get up to 500°F+, which is an extremely high heat and great for getting that nice sear on a steak. The steak goes on the grill, and due to the high temperature, it will not take long to cook the steak. For a rare steak you will need to cook it until the internal temperature is about 130°F. Since the grill is way hotter than that, you must watch the steak and time when to remove the meat from the grill. Leaving it on the grill too long will overcook the meat. If the meat stayed on the grill it would eventually reach the actual temperature of the grill itself and develop a texture something like leather. Sous vide, however, uses a completely different approach.

QUESTION

Can I cook sous vide by heating water on the stove?

Not really, because sous vide machines are built to maintain a consistent temperature with very little variance. The stovetop elements regularly go on and off to keep adding heat to the pot. This will create too much swing in the temperature to effectively cook sous vide.

When the vacuum-sealed meat is dropped into a sous vide water bath, the temperature of the water is the same as the target temperature of the meat. Therefore, if you want a juicy medium-rare strip loin steak, the temperature of the water will be around 134°F. Sous vide machines are precise and control the temperature very well, holding it at 134°F for the entire cooking time. While the meat will obviously take longer to come to the target internal temperature of 134°F, since the heat around it is much lower than that of the grill, once it reaches the target temperature, it will not overcook. While it sounds crazy, this is completely true. A steak can be completely cooked and reach 134°F in 1 hour, but it can stay in the water bath for many more hours and not overcook. Instead, it will be held at that medium-rare doneness the entire time. When ready, simply pull the bag from the water bath and remove the steak from the bag. If desired, give it a very quick sear on a hot skillet and it is ready to eat.

Sous vide is great for cooking more than just steak. It can cook a chicken breast so that it is tender and juicy with no fear of it drying out. This is an excellent way to cook a wonderful fillet of salmon or make pulled pork so that it is moist and fall-apart tender. Sous vide is also a great way to cook vegetables and so much more. This method is simple, convenient, and almost foolproof.

Isn't This Just a Fancy Way to Boil in a Bag?

At first glance, many people look at *sous vide* and think that it is essentially just a new term for "boil in a bag" cooking. Most commonly seen with rice, "boil in the bag" cooking has found a niche with some people, and you can easily find a box of Uncle Ben's Boil-in-Bag Rice on most major supermarket shelves. In fact, campers have long used freezer bags and vacuum sealer bags to quickly and easily reheat meals while out in the wilderness. It is quite convenient.

Is sous vide cooking the same as this? There are some similarities between these two techniques; for example, they both vacuum seal food in a bag and cook it in hot water, but that is where the similarities end. Sous vide cooking is all about precision and consistency of temperature. Sous vide cooking uses the understanding that by cooking meat (and other foods) at the exact desired finished internal temperature, there will be significant benefits in both taste and texture. While the main purpose of "boil in a bag" is convenience, the main reason most people use sous vide is because of the incredible improvement in taste. At the same time, sous vide does also make life in the kitchen easier and there are some serious bonus advantages to using this method.

Uncovering the History of Sous Vide

There are two chefs who played a significant role in the early stages of sous vide cooking. These pioneers each contributed to the development of this new and refined way of cooking. Vacuum sealing food had been used for decades, but these chefs took this knowledge and practice to the next culinary level.

In the early 1970s, Chef Bruno Goussault was seeking a way to cook tougher cuts of beef. He discovered that if beef was vacuum sealed and then cooked in a water bath, set at a lower cooking temperature, it resulted in a finished product that had an enhanced taste and texture. On top of that, Chef Goussault also discovered that there is reduced shrinkage when beef is cooked this way.

Around the same time Chef Georges Pralus, at the request of the restaurant Troisgros in France, was seeking to cook foie gras in such a way that it would retain its shape and texture as well as maximize its flavor. Chef Pralus discovered that if the foie gras is wrapped in multiple layers of plastic wrap and then cooked in a water bath it has an improved taste and texture.

From these early pioneers, sous vide quickly became a common cooking method in restaurants and commercial kitchens. Over time, others like Chef Heston Blumenthal of the Fat Duck in Bray, Berkshire, England, and Chef Thomas Keller of the French Laundry in the Napa Valley of California, further raised the profile of sous vide cooking. Books like *Under Pressure: Cooking Sous Vide*, by Thomas Keller, and *Modernist Cuisine: The Art of Science and Cooking*, by Nathan Myhrvold, Chris Young, and Maxime Bilet, were published, which provided lots of information and recipes regarding sous vide.

Eventually, foodies began to try and use the sous vide cooking technique at home. Since the machines available were primarily for commercial kitchens, the prices tended to be out of reach for most home cooks. Getting creative, some do-it-yourself instructions began to pop up on the Internet, showing ways for home cooks to modify rice cookers or slow cookers into sous vide machines using PID (proportional-integral-derivative) controllers. While complicated, it was a way for culinary enthusiasts to take a crack at sous vide cooking.

In recent years, companies like PolyScience and SousVide Supreme have made sous vide cooking appliances specifically targeted for home kitchens. These are smaller in size and lower in cost than the commercial models. After that, other companies began to release other sous vide machines. Some of these companies, like Nomiku, Anova, and Sansaire, used Kickstarter to successfully crowdfund their project. These products made sous vide realistic and affordable for the home cook.

Today, while sous vide is still considered a new culinary trend, it does have a solid history and is really establishing itself in home kitchens all over the world. Many people regard sous vide as the best way to cook tender meat like steaks, chicken breasts, salmon, and more. In addition, sous vide has revolutionized the process of cooking tougher cuts of meat so that they are tender and succulent.

The Benefits of Cooking Sous Vide

In any home kitchen, there are multiple ways to cook meat or vegetables. They can be roasted in the oven or cooked on the stovetop using methods like pan-searing, boiling, or steaming. Along with these methods, there are microwaves, deep fryers, grills, and smokers. With so many different cooking processes, it is understandable that you might look at sous vide with apprehension and a feeling of "do I really need another appliance?"

To fully understand sous vide, it is important to grasp the benefits that come with using this cooking process. While many different types of food can be cooked sous vide including vegetables, fruit, dessert, and even eggs, the most popular thing to cook in a sous vide water bath is meat. Sous vide just shines when it comes to cooking meat.

Perfectly Cooked Meat

Purchasing an expensive cut of meat can cause fear and trepidation, as people worry about overcooking or undercooking it. This is completely understandable. Who wants to spend lots of hard-earned money for a quality Wagyu rib eye steak, only to overcook it? This is one place where sous vide cooking excels, because the temperature-controlled water bath can ensure that the steak is cooked exactly as you like it. Set the temperature and walk away: that is it! Once it has cooked the designated time, it is done and ready to eat.

Even some cuts of meat that are challenging to cook well, like lamb chops or duck breasts, are incredibly simple with sous vide. Where these meats go from perfectly cooked to overcooked in a matter of minutes when using traditional cooking methods, there is no fear of that with sous vide. Instead, due to the precision of the temperature-controlled water, the meat is cooked to that temperature perfectly, every time.

QUESTION

Is sous vide meat generally undercooked?

Not at all. Food safety is very important. Eliminating pathogens in meat is fairly scientific and is measured by a combination of temperature and time. It is possible to kill pathogens in meat by cooking at some lower temperatures and holding the meat at that temperature for a longer period of time.

Oh So Tender

Since the water bath is heated to the target temperature of the meat, it is possible to hold it at that temperature for many more hours after the meat is cooked. This provides a significant benefit for tougher cuts of meat. Pork shoulder, beef short ribs, and other cuts of meat need a longer cook time to break down the collagen and connective tissues. Sous vide can do this easily, and there are some incredible recipes that use these cuts of meat to create something absolutely delicious.

There are even some recipes that cook meat in the sous vide for more than a day. Yes, you read that right: *more* than a day. If you check around online, you'll see that there are even recipes that call for meat to be cooked in the sous vide for up to 72 hours. While this does tenderize the meat, some actually feel that cooking it for this long actually makes it a little on the mushy side. Typically, 24–36 hours is more than plenty to tenderize even the toughest cuts of meat.

ALERT

> As with any form of cooking, it is important to follow the proper food safety guidelines. This cookbook is just a reference and anyone cooking sous vide needs to understand and follow FDA and USDA guidelines for cooking meat according to the correct combination of temperature and time. See *Appendix A: Time and Temperature Charts*.

More Than Just Meat

While sous vide is most often praised for how well it can cook a steak or a rack of lamb, it is also a wonderful way to cook other foods. Cooking vegetables in the sous vide provides a nice firm texture to the vegetables, preventing them from going all mushy. It is also possible to cook sauces and custards in the sous vide. Crème anglaise and hollandaise sauce are great examples of other recipes to make in the water bath, as the lower temperature can ensure that the eggs do not cook, but instead gently heat, creating a super-creamy texture. Also, there is nothing that can prepare you for the amazing experience that is eating your first sous vide egg. The water bath is able to cook an egg in such a way that it is soft and almost custard-like. Sous vide eggs are ideal for eggs Benedict, hash, and Japanese noodle soup.

Time Not So Much of a Factor

The sous vide makes it nearly impossible to overcook most cuts of meat. Since the meat can stay in the water bath for hours past the cook time, it makes cooking far more convenient. It is possible to start some meat in the sous vide before you leave for work, and it will be ready once you arrive home. Since meat can typically stay in the water bath longer, if traffic is bad on the way home from work, there is usually no need to worry. The sous vide can hold the meat at that temperature until you arrive home and are ready to eat.

In the same way, if dinner guests are running late, there is no fear of the meat overcooking and drying out. If your are having a nice conversation with your guests and want to push the meal back another 30 minutes, the sous vide can usually let that happen with little to no problem.

ESSENTIAL

> While many different meats like beef, pork, chicken, and more can stay in the sous vide water bath longer than the minimum time, this does not work as well with seafood. For example, the texture of salmon, shrimp, and scallops can all be negatively affected by cooking longer than the set time.

Many people find this benefit of sous vide cooking to be liberating, as it significantly reduces stress around mealtime. There is no fear of the meat overcooking, as it is in the water bath ready to go when you are.

Fine Dining at Home

Sous vide cooking provides so many opportunities for home cooks to expand their culinary skills and prepare food in ways that seemed impossible before. Sous vide makes cooking some fine-dining dishes more accessible and simplifies complicated cooking tasks. Whether it is making a succulent *Halibut with Sicilian Ragu* (Chapter 11) or *Steak and Scallops with Chipotle Cream* (Chapter 9), the sous vide is ready to stretch the home cook into new and exciting culinary realms.

It makes sense that you may look at many new kitchen tools as simply a gadget that is "here one day and gone the next." There are countless examples of these contraptions packed away in closets and garages everywhere. Many of these tools are just gimmicks and nothing more. That is not the case with sous vide, as it is so much more than some gizmo to fill up your kitchen. Sous vide is truly an innovation in the way that you cook, and it is a culinary trend that will be here for years to come.

Chapter 2
The Necessary Equipment

Starting the adventure of sous vide cooking is exciting, but it can also be overwhelming. This culinary technique is not only a new way to cook, but it also requires specific equipment. Some equipment is essential, while there are a few optional tools that can be helpful for the home cook.

Sous Vide Machines

The first thing that a sous vide newbie needs is some way to heat and control the temperature of a water bath. Sous vide cooking is all about precision. When food is placed in a water bath, it is essential that there is very little swing above or below the set temperature. Temperature swing is not as critical when cooking on the stovetop, oven, or grill, but in sous vide cooking, it is crucial because the temperature of the water is set to be the target temperature of the meat.

QUESTION

What kind of sous vide machine should I buy?

A water oven is a great choice if you will use it often and have room on the counter. These are quiet and typically can cook a lot of food at once. Immersion circulators are lower in price, smaller in size, a great choice for smaller kitchens or portability option, and just as effective at heating and maintaining water temperature.

A number of years ago, if someone wanted to get into sous vide cooking at home, there were few options. It was either spend lots of money for a commercial unit or build your own contraption. Today, there are many different choices that range in price, quality, design, and functionality.

Water Ovens

One type of sous vide machine available for the home cook is a water oven. These all-in-one machines are convenient and ideal for someone wanting a unit that both holds and heats water. These units contain a large water reservoir for cooking sous vide. The control panel on a water oven allows you to set the water temperature, and some models have timers on them as well. There are not a lot of different companies that sell sous vide water ovens designed for the home kitchen. By far, the most popular and well known is by SousVide Supreme.

A SousVide Supreme water oven

Setting temperature on a SousVide Supreme water oven

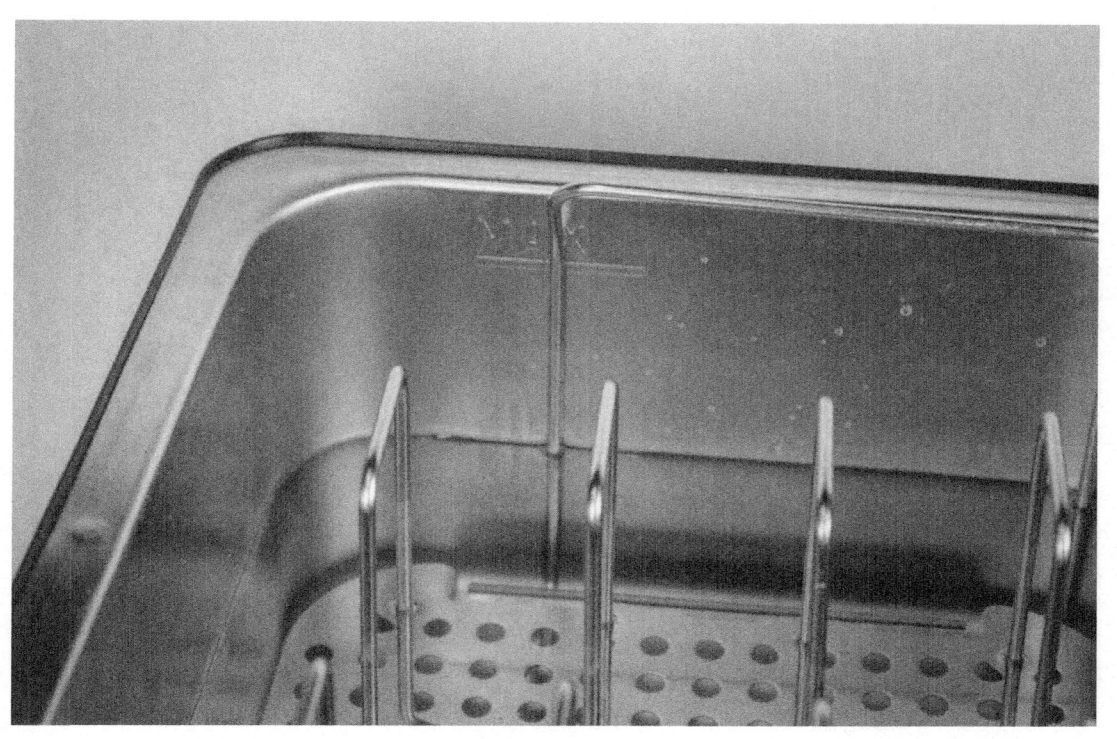

SousVide Supreme water-level line

SousVide Supreme water tank

    Typically, the heating element in water ovens is underneath the reservoir, which allows for even and steady heating. As the water is heated at the bottom of the reservoir, it rises to ensure consistent and level temperatures throughout the water bath. Vacuum-sealed bags of food are placed in the reservoir either horizontally or vertically and the water surrounds the bags to provide even heating. Some water ovens come with a rack that is ideal for ensuring that the bags of food are evenly placed and never touching. A rack also maximizes the space in the water bath, since many bags of food can be lined up side by side.

Water ovens have some significant advantages over the other sous vide models and methods. For example, water ovens come with all that you need to get started cooking sous vide, as they hold the water and also heat the water. Most of the other sous vide machine options require additional tools or devices, and some other sous vide methods actually require the modification of equipment. Since this can be a bit overwhelming, the water oven is a great choice for anyone entering into this new culinary adventure of sous vide.

The design of a water oven is typically quite simple and there are little to no moving parts, so there is not much externally that can either break or require maintenance. Most water ovens use very little energy compared to some of the other sous vide options available. The water oven is an ideal choice if you plan to cook sous vide regularly. A typical water oven is the size of a small microwave, so it will take up a lot of space on the countertop.

Immersion Circulators

Over the past couple of years, as sous vide has grown significantly in popularity, a number of new machines have hit the market. Of these units, the most common type is the sous vide immersion circulator. Specifically designed for the home kitchen, immersion circulators have been developed by both established companies and brand-new entrepreneurs. PolyScience is one company that has been in the sous vide market for years, providing machines for restaurants and commercial kitchens. Recently, PolyScience has released models of its immersion circulators made for the home kitchen. In addition there have been some other companies that have used crowdfunding methods, like Kickstarter, to raise the initial investment to launch its product. Nomiku and

Anova are two such companies, and they each have popular immersion circulators on the market.

A PolyScience immersion circulator

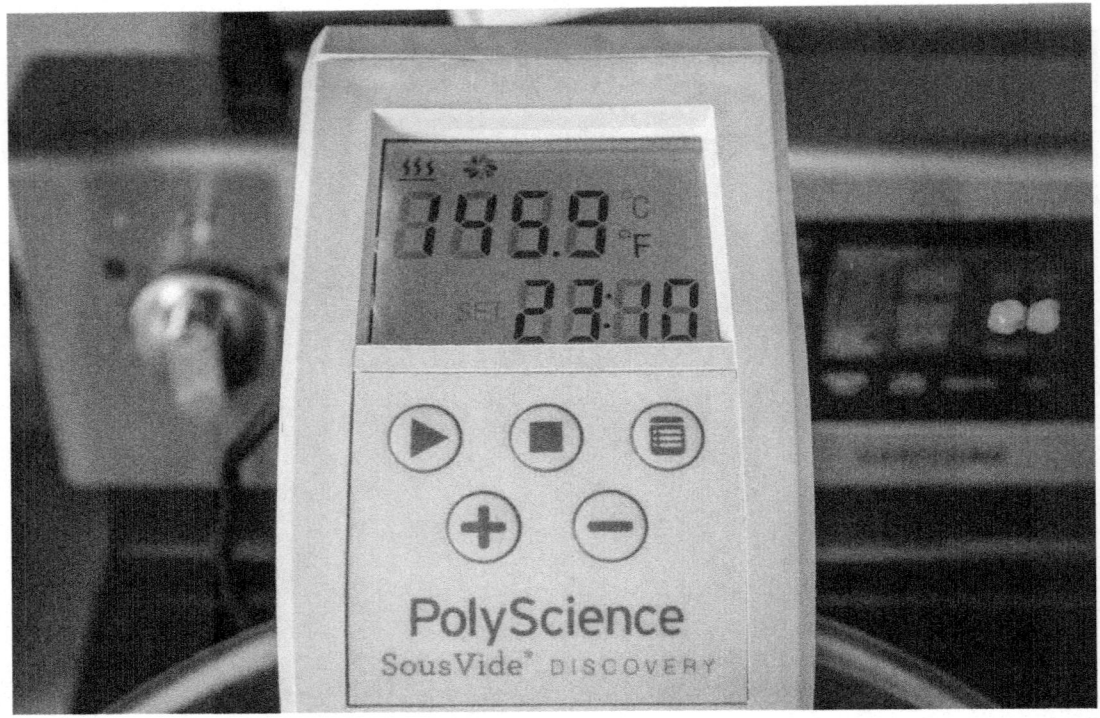

The control panel for a PolyScience immersion circulator

A PolyScience immersion circulator at water level. Be sure to fill the pot to the minimum water line, and do no overfill past the maximum water line.

An Anova immersion circulator

Immersion circulators are different from water ovens in that they are not an all-in-one unit. The immersion circulator clamps on to a large pot, polycarbonate tank, cooler, or other container holding the water. Part of the immersion circulator rests inside the water bath and within this section of the machine there are a few internal parts. There is a thermometer continually measuring the temperature of the water. Along with that there is a heating unit that warms up the water to the designated temperature. There is also a pump or impeller that circulates the water. This pump is an important part of these machines, as a constant movement of water throughout the tank ensures that there is a steady temperature throughout the water bath and that there are no cold pockets.

FACT

While many new immersion circulator home units have hit the market over the past few years, it is by no means a new style of machine. Restaurants and other commercial kitchens have been using immersion circulators for years and, in many cases, these machines have been an integral part of their cooking equipment.

The entire immersion circulator is not immersed; usually more than half the machine is above the water. This section holds the electrical components, on/off switch, control panel, and display. From here, the user can set and monitor the desired temperature of the water bath. Typically, immersion circulators also include a timer that can be set for how long you want the machine to stay on. Some newer immersion circulators are even Wi-Fi enabled, utilizing mobile apps for greater control.

Immersion circulators are an excellent choice when looking to invest in a sous vide system. They can be more economical than a water oven and they are perfect for cooking enough food for the average family or even for a dinner party. On top of that, one of the great aspects of an immersion circulator is its size. It will not take up a lot of space on the countertop and can be stored when not in use. The fact that an immersion circulator can turn a large stockpot into a water oven is advantageous for the person with a small kitchen who does not want another big appliance.

A close-up of multiple immersion circulators. Note that the maximum and minimum water levels vary by brand.

DIY Machines

Early on, when foodies started to discover the culinary benefits of sous vide cooking, they tried to create ways to cook this way at home. A quick search online will reveal many different do-it-yourself methods for building a home sous vide machine.

Some designs use rice cookers or slow cookers as the water bath and to heat the water. In these cases, an external thermostat is built in or attached to the cooker to monitor and regulate the temperature. Since sous vide cooking requires precise temperature control, a digital PID (proportional-integral-derivative) controller is used to tell the rice cooker or slow cooker when to heat and when to stop. There are a number of PID controllers available online that can be used for these types of sous vide systems. Also, there are some detailed instructions online that show how to build a temperature controller from cheap parts.

One other way that engineer savvy foodies have created sous vide machines is by designing and building their own immersion circulator. From a collection of cheap parts available online, people have built devices that heat water to a certain temperature and circulate the water with aquarium pumps. These machines are clever designs and can be quite effective.

ALERT

These do-it-yourself machines do raise questions and concerns about their reliability at controlling precise temperature over a long period of time. While these may be fun "hobby" machines, purchasing one of the professionally built machines on the market is a much safer way to cook.

Over the last few years, many new sous vide machines have become available that are specifically designed for the home. These cost much less than the commercial machines and have a smaller, sleeker design for the home kitchen. The availability of these machines has made the do-it-yourself option far less appealing. These new store-bought sous vide units are only slightly more expensive than one built from scratch, and they have many advantages. Not only do purchased machines look nicer than anything that could be built at home, but they have also been designed, built, and tested by companies that specialize in this type of equipment. That provides a degree of safety and assurance that is important when cooking food.

A Cooler, a Kettle, and a Thermometer

Easily, the simplest method of creating a sous vide unit is by using a cooler. Also known as ice chests or ice boxes, these portable coolers are insulated to keep food and drinks cold. Whether it is for a picnic, a trip to the beach, or a simple outdoor party, people have used these portable coolers for years. While traditionally used to keep food chilled, it is also possible to use the coolers for sous vide cooking, as the inside can become a large water bath. Using a cooler for sous vide is generally quite simple and it uses equipment most people already own. All that is needed to get going is a kettle, a thermometer, and obviously, a cooler.

There are many different types of coolers on the market. Typically, they are made with inner and outer shells of plastic with hard foam insulation in between. There are also coolers that have an outer shell made of galvanized metal or aluminum, and there are even disposable coolers made of polystyrene foam. An excellent cooler for sous vide is the smaller beer coolers, which are the perfect size for cooking a steak.

To get things started, fill the cooler with hot tap water and set the thermometer in the water. The best kind of digital thermometer to use is one with a long probe and cable. This way, the probe can be inside the cooler, resting in the water, while the thermometer display is outside. Doing this allows the water temperature to be monitored while the cooler lid is closed. It is best to have the thermometer as close to the center of the water bath as possible. If using this kind of thermometer is not possible, then a standard, instant-read thermometer will also work fine. Fill the kettle with water and bring it to a boil. Once the water comes to a boil, pour some into the cooler until it reaches the desired temperature for sous vide cooking. It is helpful to start with the temperature being 5°F–10°F higher than the desired target food temperature since there will be a fast drop once the food is added.

ALERT

There is no way to guarantee that the temperature is even throughout in a cooler and there are greater temperature swings that will happen as the water cools and is reheated by pouring in hotter water. This may be okay for some shorter recipes like a thin fish fillet or possibly a 1"-thick steak, but chicken, pork, and other long sous vide sessions are not recommended.

At this stage, the vacuum-sealed or zip-top pouches of food can be added to the water bath in the cooler. Cover the lid and monitor the temperature. There usually is a quick drop in temperature immediately after the pouches are added to the water. Whenever necessary, add some boiling water from the kettle to the cooler. One helpful tip is to use a wooden spoon to stir the water every once in a while. This will ensure that the water temperature is consistent throughout the water bath and that there are no pockets of hot or cold water. Any time the water drops 1 or 2 degrees below the target temperature, stir in a bit more boiling water to bring it back up to the target temperature. After cooking the designated length of time according to the chart in Appendix A, check the core temperature when it comes out of the water. If it has not reached the target internal temperature, it should go back in for longer.

This cooler method is definitely not a substitute for using an actual sous vide machine. Using the cooler method requires far more monitoring and manual adjustment than any of the other ways to cook sous vide. There can also be more hot or cold water pockets, since there is neither even circulation within the water nor even heating throughout the unit. Purchasing a sous vide machine can seem expensive if you've never cooked using this culinary technique, so the cooler method allows you to experiment with it, taste the results, and decide whether you want to buy a machine.

Vacuum Sealers and Food-Safe Bags

Sous vide is a French term meaning "under pressure," so the premise of this cooking technique requires that the food be in a bag with all the air drawn out. This means that as the bag of food is immersed in the temperature-controlled water bath, there is no air in between the hot water and the food. This is extremely important, as any air will impact the temperature and cooking time of the food.

So, in order to cook sous vide you need a way to place the food in a bag and remove all the air. There are a number of different types of products that can do this and they range in price, functionality, and effectiveness.

Standard Suction-Type Vacuum Sealer

Of all the vacuum-sealing methods and machines available, the suction type is by far the most common type used in home kitchens. There are many different suction-type vacuum sealers on the market from many different companies and they are available in well-known stores across the country. On top of that, the bags used are readily available and can also usually be used across brand lines.

ESSENTIAL

> While suction-type vacuum sealers struggle with lots of liquid, there are ways to work around this issue. Freeze the marinade in an ice-cube tray. Dump the frozen marinade cubes into the bag with the meat. The vacuum sealer will work great at drawing out all the air and sealing the bag. Add an extra 30–60 minutes to the cook time for the marinade to thaw.

With these types of vacuum sealers the open part of the bag is inserted into a slot and clamped down by an arm. Then the air is drawn out of the bag and it is sealed with a heat strip. These machines can effectively vacuum seal bags of many different sizes. A significant downside to these types of vacuum sealers is that they struggle with liquid. Unable to distinguish between air and liquid, they can suck out all the air and then draw liquid out of the bag. Therefore sealing meat with lots of marinade is not ideal for suction-type vacuum sealers.

Preparing ingredients in a vacuum seal bag

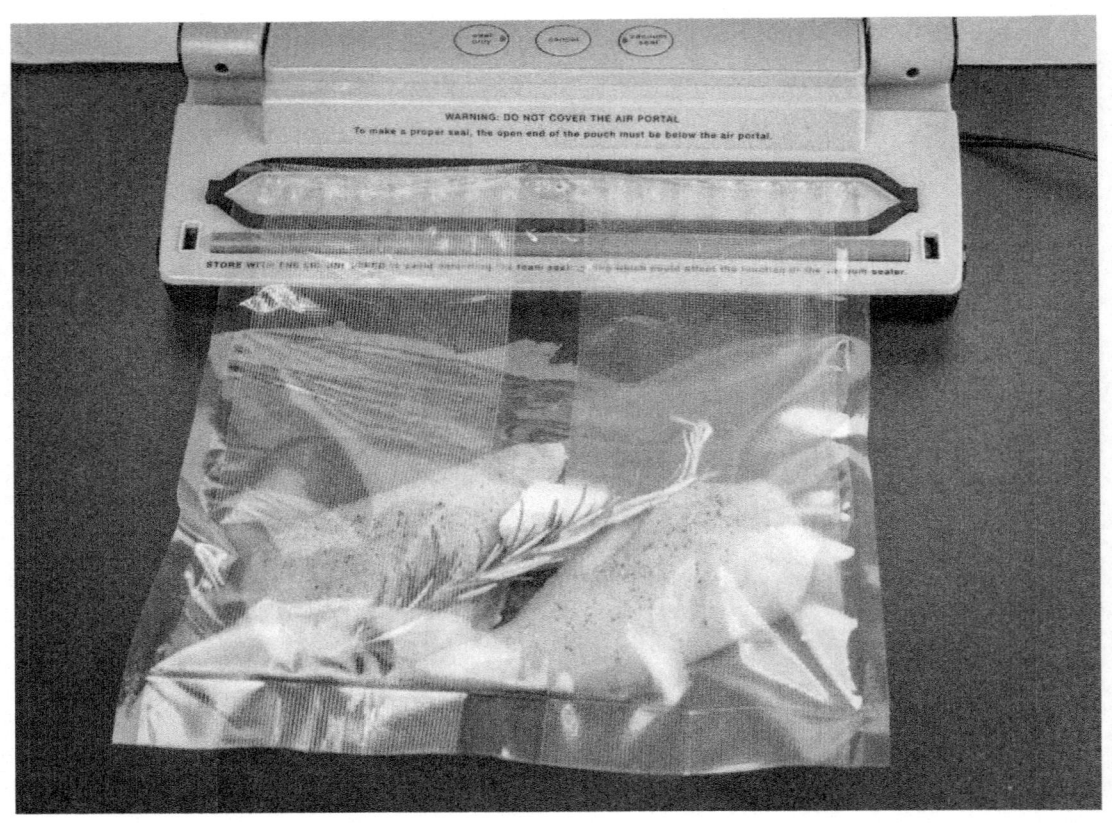

A SousVide Supreme "suction-type" vacuum sealer being prepared to start the seal

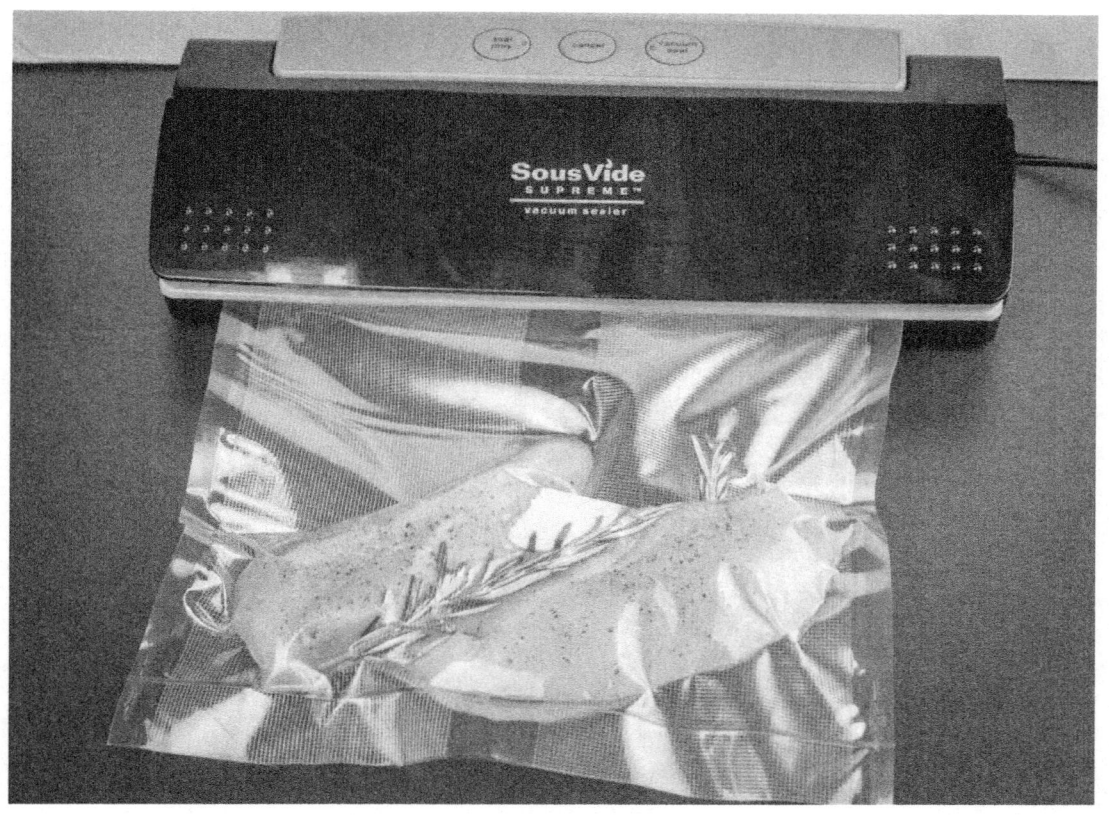

A SousVide Supreme vacuum sealer in progress

Try to place items in a single layer to ensure even cooking.

Suction-type bags work best when ingredients do not have lots of marinade or liquid surrounding them.

Cubed pork roast being prepared in a FoodSaver vacuum sealer

Ingredients being prepared in a chamber vacuum sealer

Chamber Vacuum Sealers

The chamber vacuum sealer works with a very different technique than the suction-type model. Food is placed in a food-safe bag and then put into a "chamber." The door/lid of the machine is closed with the entire bag in this chamber space. Once the vacuum sealer is initialized, air is pulled out of the chamber and it is pressurized. Once the air is drawn out of the chamber, the heat strip seals the bag. Then the air is drawn back into the chamber and the lid can be lifted.

Chamber vacuums are significantly more effective than suction-type machines, and they work just fine with liquid. Chamber vacuums are so good at sealing liquid in a bag that it is even possible to vacuum seal a bag of soup. With most chamber vacuums it is also possible to adjust how much air is pulled out of the chamber. This is great for vacuum sealing delicate food like salmon.

A sealed chamber vacuum bag

The main downside of chamber vacuums is the cost, as they are significantly more expensive than standard suction-type machines. While they are pricey and usually out of reach for most home cooks, they do use food-safe bags that are much cheaper than the bags suction-type vacuum sealers use. Therefore, over time, the cost difference does balance out.

Handheld Vacuum Sealers

Another type of vacuum sealer is the handheld model. These use specialized food-safe bags that have a valve, usually in the corner of the bag. The vacuum sealer is held over the valve and then turned on. This draws the air out of the bag and the valve is sealed shut.

These machines do have some advantages over the other vacuum sealers. Handheld machines are much smaller than the larger units, so they are easy to stick in the drawer of a small kitchen. Much cheaper, these machines are an economical alternative to some of the pricier vacuum sealers on the market. The major downside of these machines is that while they may seem cheaper, they require very specific bags that are often more expensive than standard vacuum sealer bags. Therefore, these machines will end up costing more than other machines on the market that have a higher initial cost.

Zip-Top Bags

It is actually possible to use sturdy food-safe zipper bags. These bags do not work with vacuum sealers, therefore, the air is removed manually. Food is placed in the bag and the air is drawn out of the bag using the air displacement method, a process based on Archimedes' principle. To use this technique, simply place the food in the bag and do not close or zip the seal. Slowly lower the bag into the water. As the bag enters the water, it will push the air out of the bag. Water will press up against the food in the bag, creating a vacuum environment. Lower the bag so that the zipper seal is just above the water. Now press the seal to close the bag and you have a manually made vacuum-sealed bag.

ALERT

It is extremely important to use bags that are not only food-safe, but are also safe being heated. Check the manufacturer's information to learn not only whether the plastic bag can be heated, but also the length of time it can be in a hot environment like a sous vide water bath.

Many people use zip-top bags when first starting sous vide cooking. These are a great way to first get going before investing in a vacuum sealer. This method is also great for working with liquids. Where suction-type vacuum sealers struggle with liquid, the air-displacement method and these bags work fine. One issue with zipper bags is there is a chance that the seal could break and they could open up in the water bath. This seems to happen more frequently while using sous vide immersion circulators, as the water moving around in the bath causes the bags to move, increasing the chance of them opening. Make sure that the seal is fully zipped and the bag is completely sealed before lowering into the water. Some companies have zipper bags specifically designed for sous vide cooking. SousVide Supreme sells zip-cooking pouches in different sizes, and these are designed for cooking at high temperatures.

Slowly lowering zip-top bags into the water bath will force air out and create a vacuum environment.

A Nomiku immersion circulator

Optional Additional Equipment

There are a number of other pieces of equipment that can enhance and simplify sous vide cooking. While these are not essential to creating quality meals using sous vide, they can make life a little easier for the cook.

Kitchen Torch

While the recipes in this book give instructions to sear using a skillet, a kitchen torch is another effective way to sear meat after it has come out of the water bath. The extreme heat from the flame of a kitchen torch will create a Maillard reaction, resulting in a crispy and extra-tasty meat exterior. The kitchen torch can simulate a hot grill and works really well for steak, pork chops, fish, and more. There are a number of small crème brûlée torches that are great, as well as powerful cooking torches that clamp on to a butane canister. These tend to have more adjustability in the size of the flame and can get hotter.

Digital Thermometer

Sous vide machines have built-in thermostats to measure the temperature of the water, but there may be times that you want to monitor the temperature of the food. In these cases, a quality digital thermometer is in order. Instead of an instant-read thermometer, the best kind for sous vide cooking is one with a long hypodermic probe with a cable/cord that is safe to put in the water. ThermoWorks makes excellent digital thermometers and has models that are safe and effective for sous vide cooking.

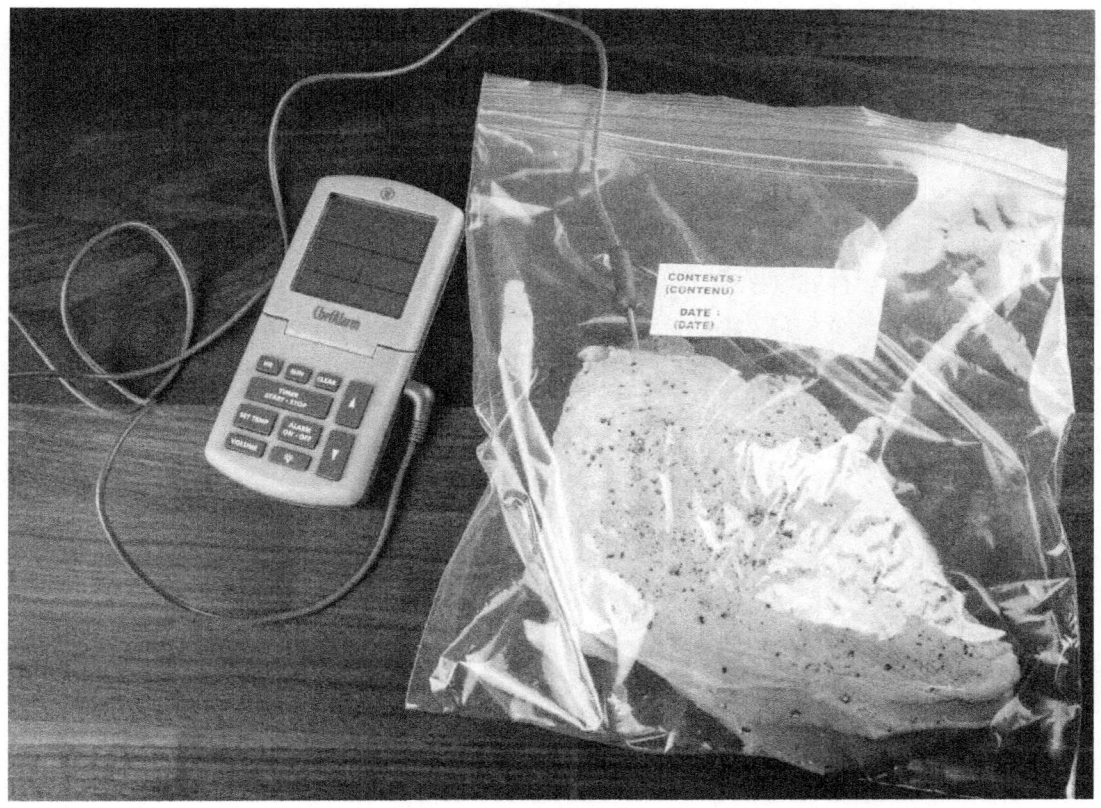

A digital thermometer with a probe and cable will help you monitor the internal temperature of your food.

Foam Tape

Piercing a digital thermometer hypodermic probe into a vacuum-sealed bag will break the seal and this can allow air and water into the bag. Placing some foam tape onto the bag and piercing through the tape into the bag will keep the seal intact. It is a cheap and effective way to ensure the food is vacuum sealed. Poly Science sells foam tape that is ideal for this purpose.

Polycarbonate Containers and Lids

Immersion circulators can be clamped on to a stockpot or cooler and work effectively, but polycarbonate containers are also an excellent choice. These containers usually hold much more water than a pot and their rectangular design is better for cooking multiple bags of food, allowing them to be evenly spaced and not crowded in a pot. Polycarbonate lids can be cut to create a hole for the immersion circulator to fit.

Chapter 3
Getting Started

There are some cooking techniques that are challenging and difficult to master. Tempering chocolate, cooking hard candy, making that perfect soufflé, or even rolling out a pie crust can be frustrating. The thought of trying a brand-new cooking method causes some people to run for the hills, because the last thing anyone needs is more frustration or more failure. It is understandable that you may feel that way about sous vide, but once you give it a go, you will discover that it is pretty darn easy! Using sous vide as a method for cooking is surprisingly simple and there are a handful of basic steps that, if followed, will produce quality results each and every time.

The General Setup

While sous vide cooking is quite the simple method, there are still a number of things to consider when getting started. Knowing is half the battle, and this chapter gives you the knowledge and tools you need, so that any anxiety or questions you may have along the way are easily answered. There are a few things to do prior to dropping a bag of food into the water bath. Nothing is arduous or tough, but following these few simple steps will make sure that you are ready to go.

Location for the Sous Vide

So, you have a sous vide and are ready to use it to cook something delicious. Where do you plan to set it up? There are some factors to consider when deciding the best place in the kitchen to set up the water bath. Obviously the size of the pot or container that will be filled with water needs to be taken into consideration. Put the water bath in a place that will not be in the way of, or interfere with, other kitchen tasks. Also, be well aware that the container will get hot as the water is heated to cook the food, except in the case of water ovens, like that of the SousVide Supreme, as they have an insulated outer shell. In most other situations, especially with immersion circulators, water will be filled in pots or polycarbonate tanks. These will get very hot and need to be resting on something that can handle prolonged heat exposure. Granite or marble countertops, stainless steel counters, and even the stovetop can all work as a good place to set the water bath. One thing to consider is to place a towel and trivet underneath the tank, as this can absorb some of the heat as it transfers through the bottom of the water bath. Make sure anything placed under the water bath is stable and does not cause rocking or movement of the tank.

QUESTION

Does water evaporate during the sous vide cooking session?

It depends on the machine. Water ovens or polycarbonate tanks with precut lids lose almost no water if the lid is on. Pots or other tanks without a lid will experience evaporation over time during a long cooking session. Simply pour in additional water to keep the level above the minimum line.

Fill Up the Tank

Filling up the tank or pot with water is one of the first things that you will need to do when getting started. With almost every sous vide machine there is a minimum and a maximum water line. The water bath needs to be within that level before turning on the machine and before placing the food bags in the bath. Water ovens, like the SousVide Supreme, have minimum and maximum indicator lines on the inside of the water tank. For immersion circulators, the indicator lines are found on the machine itself, and once the circulator is clamped on to the pot or tank, it is easy to see the required water level.

Getting Prepped

Before the food goes into the food-safe bag, it is best to make sure that everything is ready to go. Whether it is simply washing hands or chopping vegetables, it is important to get everything prepped.

Here is a list of things to do to get ready:

- Wash hands and make sure that you are using sanitary tools and environment. Rinse vegetables and anything else necessary to ensure things are clean.
- Get out the food-safe bags. This puts them within reach and also makes sure that you have enough.
- Get out all the ingredients to make sure that you have enough of everything and to ensure that all the ingredients are within reach. There is nothing more frustrating than being unable to find an ingredient in the pantry or fridge while you are in the middle of cooking.
- Trim the meat of any extra fat, membrane, and tissue. If desired or necessary, cut the meat into chunks or serving portions (this can be particularly helpful for large cuts of meat or whole salmon fillets).
- If vegetables are used in the recipe, peel, chop, or slice them so that they are ready to go.
- Measure out and mix up any marinades or spice blends for seasoning the meat or other vegetables.

The Basic Steps for Sous Vide

After you are ready to go and have all the food prepped, there are some standard steps that apply to almost every sous vide cooking session. These steps are simple, and following them will help you in the journey of sous vide.

Season

One of the most important steps in cooking is properly seasoning the food. Poorly seasoned meat or vegetables can result in food that is both bland and completely forgettable. Knowing how much to season and when to properly season can seem tricky, as there is not much worse than a piece of perfectly cooked pork that is way too salty.

ESSENTIAL

In some cases, meat is seared prior to being placed in the food-safe bag and vacuum sealed. This searing can enhance the flavor and mimic braising. It is important that the meat be cooled completely after it is seared because when hot meat is vacuum sealed it has a steaming effect on the meat when added to the sous vide water bath.

When it comes to sous vide cooking there will be times that you will want to season the meat or vegetables prior to them being vacuum sealed in a food-safe bag. Other times, you will want to vacuum seal them without any seasoning, knowing that there will be a sauce, glaze, or other seasoning added after the food comes out of the water bath. The recipes in this book include times when food is seasoned first and examples when it is seasoned after. Both can work well depending on the dish.

Here are a few tips regarding seasoning meat:

- Some seasoning includes a spice blend that is rubbed all over the meat. To maximize flavor, make sure that every part of the meat is rubbed down with the spices.
- Fresh herbs are wonderful and they can have a strong impact on the meat. A small sprig of thyme or rosemary can really enhance a chicken breast, pork chop, or other cut of meat.
- Marinades can be an excellent way to season the meat. Adding a little bit of honey garlic sauce, homemade marinade, or even a few squirts of barbecue sauce with the meat can provide enhanced flavor.
- Not much liquid is needed for a marinade and it is best to minimize how much is used. A lot of liquid can make sealing the bag difficult, particularly if using an edge vacuum sealer. Also, if a lot of liquid is surrounding the meat in the bag, it can impact the actual cooking, requiring more time for the meat to cook through.
- Although adding alcohol like beer or wine can infuse a wonderful flavor to the meat, it can also cause a bitter taste in the meat. To solve this, simply boil off the alcohol from the beer, wine, or other liquor in a saucepan. Then let it cool completely before pouring it into the food-safe bag with the meat.

Marinades are great ways to season meat and add moisture and flavor during the sous vide cooking process.

FACT

> Now, while there may not be scientific proof for this, it seems that less seasoning is needed when vacuum sealing meat. It could be that the pressured environment enhances the flavor and improves how it infuses into the meat. So, the "less is more" philosophy is sometimes helpful, and don't forget, more seasoning can always be added later.

Meat is not the only food that can be seasoned before it is sealed in the food-safe bag. Vegetables are amazing cooked in the sous vide and one of the impressive aspects of this cooking technique is that aromatics are easily infused into the cooked vegetables.

Seal

Once the meat or vegetables have been seasoned, they are ready to be bagged and sealed. Typically, a special food-safe bag is used, and then a vacuum sealer removes the air and seals the bag with a heat bar on the vacuum sealer. Remember, sous vide is French for "under vacuum," and this vacuum sealing of the food is standard to the sous vide practice. It is essential that the air be removed from the bag, as air will lift the bag out of the water. Air also prevents the temperature-controlled water from being pressed up against the meat or other food, which is necessary for proper sous vide cooking.

QUESTION

Does all the air need to be removed from the bag?

It may be impossible to remove all the air with certain foods. When vacuum sealing carrots it is pretty much impossible to get all the air out because the carrots will not all be perfectly flush side by side. That is okay, as long as most of the air is gone. It is more important for meat to have as much of the air removed as possible.

Here are a few tips for bagging and sealing the food:

- Make sure that everything is clean and sanitary. This includes your hands and any tongs or other utensils that will be transferring food into the bag.
- Folding over the top of the bag is helpful when adding meat or other food to the bag. It means that the tongs or spatula do not have to reach into the bag as far. Also, folding the top of the bag can keep it clean from any marinade or other bits of food, which is extremely helpful for ensuring that the vacuum sealer makes a clean seal.
- Make sure that the food is in one layer and as close to an even thickness as possible. Meat that is piled in the bag or stacked will not cook evenly or properly. Line pork chops, beef steaks, or chicken breasts side by side or use smaller bags and package them separately.

While it is possible to use food-safe zipper bags, make sure that they are the kind that are safe to be heated for the length of time that they will be in the sous vide water bath. These types of bags are good for recipes that have a fair amount of liquid, like the pickle and relish recipes in this book.

Here are the steps for getting air out of the zipper bags:

- Place the ingredients in a food-safe zipper bag.
- Slowly lower the bag into the water using the water displacement method; the air will escape from the bag.
- Continue to lower the bag until it is about 1" from being fully submerged.
- Once the bag has been lowered, just zip it shut with your fingers.

Once the food has been sealed, it can be placed in the fridge until it is ready to be cooked sous vide. The first two steps (season and seal) can be done in advance of when the food will be cooked. This is advantageous for a dinner party, holiday meal, or other event, as it is possible to prep the food, season it, and vacuum seal it in the morning or even the night before. Then, closer to dinnertime, the bags are ready to go and can be submerged in the water bath when it is time for them to start cooking.

Set

The next step in sous vide, after seasoning the food and sealing it into a bag, is to set the water bath to the desired cooking temperature. Use the *Time and Temperature Charts*, found in Appendix A, to determine the proper temperature for setting the sous vide machine. While cooking meat in an oven uses pretty standard temperatures (often 350°F or 375°F), sous vide is much more precise. The temperature of the water is set to be the desired internal temperature of the meat. Therefore, if you like your steak medium-rare, then a temperature of 134°–140°F will cook the steak so it is pink, just the way you like it. If you are cooking green beans, then setting the sous vide machine to a temperature of 183°F will be hot enough to cook the vegetables so they are tender, yet have a little snap to them.

FACT

Depending on the cooking temperature, it may take longer for the water to heat up than it does to prep the food, season it, and vacuum seal it in the food-safe bag. If you will be bagging the food just before it goes into the sous vide water bath, consider setting the temperature and getting the sous vide going at the start so that once the food is sealed, the water will be hot and ready to go.

Sous vide is all about precision, and the temperature of the water can have an enormous impact on the food, depending on what is being cooked. For example, +/–1°F can really change the texture of a soft-boiled egg and the creaminess of the yolk. In the same way, there is a great deal of personal preference regarding the texture and taste of meat, in particular. Tasting a chicken breast or salmon cooked at a lower temperature for longer may amaze some people, while others prefer the texture of these meats cooked at a higher temperature so they are closer to the traditional way.

It is essential to make sure that the water has reached the set temperature before adding the bagged food into the water bath.

Since sous vide cooking is all about precision, placing food into the bath as the water is still preheating disturbs the whole process, and you cannot be sure that the food is cooked when the time is done.

Swim

Once the water bath has finished preheating and comes to the set temperature, it is time to drop the bags into the water. Gently drop them in, so that water does not splash around. It is possible to place more than one sealed bag of food into the water bath and, depending on the size of the tank/container, it is possible to have multiple bags of meat all cooking at once in the same sous vide water bath. Some restaurants have very large water baths with many steaks, racks of lamb, or other meats cooking away.

There are a few tips and other things to consider:

- Make sure that the bags are fully submerged in the water. Try to leave at least 1" or more of water between the top of the bag and the surface of the water bath. If some of the bag is sticking out of the water bath during the cooking session it can be extremely dangerous from a food safety standpoint.
- Make sure that water is surrounding all the food in the bag. This means that the food should not be pressed up against the side of the tank or pot and that multiple bags should not be touching or pressed up against each other. For example, if two steaks are packaged separately, in two different bags, and both are in the water bath, make sure that the steaks are not resting side by side against each other.
- Consider using special sous vide racks. These racks are great for holding bagged food steady and secure under the water. It is especially advantageous when cooking multiple bags of food

at once because the rack will hold the bags in place and ensure that there is a channel of water in between the bags of food.
- This may be obvious, but make sure that if cooking multiple bags at once that they are all supposed to be cooking at the same temperature.

Sear

After the meat or other food has cooked the allotted length in the sous vide water bath, it is ready to come out of the bag to be served. While sous vide does an amazing job cooking meat so that it is tender, when it comes out of the bag it can look limp, have a grayish color, and have a soft wet exterior. This is definitely not the desired texture or even visual appearance for most cooked meats.

ALERT

Do not walk away while searing meat. Since searing is to be done at very high temperatures, the searing happens quite quickly, and depending on the cut of meat, is finished anywhere from 30 seconds up to a maximum of 2 minutes. Leaving the meat in the hot skillet too long can ruin all that hard work done in the sous vide.

To solve this issue, an excellent way to "finish" the meat and get it ready for plating and serving is to quickly sear the outside. Searing the meat will create a Maillard reaction that will give it the classic browned appearance of grilled or seared meat. On top of the visual impact, searing the meat will improve the texture and taste immensely.

The first step in searing the meat, once it has been taken out of the bag, is to pat it dry with a paper towel. Having a dry surface on the meat is an extremely important aspect to effectively creating a nice seared outer surface. If the meat is wet, it will almost steam instead of searing, so give it a quick pat with a paper towel before it is seared.

Here are a few different ways to sear meat:

- The most common way to finish off the meat is to sear it in a hot skillet. Simply heat up a skillet, over high heat, with 1–2 tablespoons of oil so that it is very hot. The oil needs to be a kind that has a high smoke point: peanut, sunflower, corn, vegetable, and safflower oils all work fine. Once the oil is hot and shimmering (it may even start smoking a little bit), gently lay the steak or other meat in the pan. Place the meat in slowly as this will both prevent the oil from splattering and keep the meat from sticking to the pan. After about 1–2 minutes, flip the meat over and sear the other side.
- Another common way that sous vide enthusiasts finish off the meat is to sear it using a kitchen torch. The flame from a kitchen torch gets very hot and it is an effective way to get a nice charred look on the outside of the meat. It finishes the meat so that it looks like it was cooked on the grill but does not continue to cook the inside of the meat.
- Another method for searing meat is to use the oven. Setting the oven to broil can put a lot of heat in the oven and it can be an excellent way to put a sear on the surface of a bunch of pork ribs. It is an excellent way to finish off pork carnitas.
- The grill is one more method for searing meat. To use the grill, make sure that it is extremely hot and that there has been

enough time for the grill grates to heat up. Brushing down the grill grates with oil will help put those appealing grill marks on the meat. Be careful though: only 1–2 minutes is needed per side, as any longer can cause the meat to cook further.

Once the meat has been seared, it can be seasoned with a little bit of salt, pepper, or other spices before being plated and served. Also, using a sauce, compound butter, or glaze can further enhance the flavor of the meat.

Searing steak in a cast-iron skillet is a great way to create the Maillard reaction and caramelize the outside of the meat.

Quickly sautéing pork belly in a nonstick skillet will crisp the edges and enhance the flavors.

Sear meat carefully in hot oil to prevent splattering.

Food Safety

Anytime food is involved there is a concern about food safety. It is important to take care regarding what you consume, because food-borne illnesses can greatly impact your health and, in some extreme cases, be fatal. Knowledge, and taking proper precautions, is the best way to guard against food-related health concerns.

Plastic and Food-Safe Bags

In this day and age of people moving away from plastic and using glass or stainless steel more often for storing or cooking foods, it is understandable that questions and concerns arise regarding the use of plastic bags. Not only is the food vacuum sealed in the bag, but it is also cooked in the bag, sometimes for hours. Look around your kitchen and you will realize that plastic is everywhere. We use plastic with food regularly, so this is not something unique to sous vide cooking. Food is packaged in bags all the time, including meat, vegetables, condiments, juices, and more.

QUESTION

Can the bags be reused again?

No, bags should not be reused for another sous vide cooking session. Since they were used to cook meat or other food, one can never be sure that they have been thoroughly cleaned, especially in the corners and crevices of the bags. It is best to just throw them in the garbage or rinse and place them in the recycling bin.

It is essential that the bags are safe for cooking at sous vide temperatures and lengths of time and that they are made with plastics free of a number of harmful chemicals and toxins. BPA (bisphenol A) and phthalates are two chemicals that are dangerous if leached into food or anything you consume. This definitely applies to sous vide cooking and it is important to make sure that proper plastics are being used. Many brand-name vacuum seal bags and zipper lock food bags manufactured and sold in the United States and Canada use plastic that is free of these harmful chemicals. These bags meet FDA standards and are safe for sous vide cooking. If there is concern regarding any particular bag or company, the best thing to do is to contact the company directly and ask them what is in their plastic bags and how they are made.

Cooking Safely

Food safety is important with any cooking method. Bacteria and pathogens can be on or in food that has been cooked in the oven, on the grill, in the smoker, or even in the deep fryer. It is important for the home cook to understand food safety and take precautions to prevent the multiplication of harmful bacteria. Sous vide is not immune from these food safety issues. In fact, because the temperatures are lower than traditional cooking, it is essential that home cooks take proper safeguards to ensure that they are caring for and cooking food properly.

The "danger zone" refers to the temperature range between 40°F and 140°F. It is termed the danger zone because bacteria and other pathogens multiply at a rapid rate in this range. The longer it takes for the cooking process to move meat through this range, the greater the risk there is in food being contaminated with hazardous bacteria such as salmonella, E. coli, listeria, and *Clostridium botulinum*. These are serious pathogens that can cause a wide range of illnesses from issues as minor as a fever or an upset stomach to serious health problems.

People often think of food safety and the reduction of pathogens in relation to a certain temperature. In many recipes and instructions on food packages, it will say to cook food to a specific internal temperature. Although cooking to that specific internal temperature will make the food safe, that is only part of the story. Time is also a factor, along with temperature, for reducing pathogens and making food safe. So, this means that meat can be cooked to a lower internal temperature and it can be deemed safe to eat if it is held at this lower temperature (or above) for a longer period of time.

ALERT

All this information is a guide, and in no way is it meant to cover all aspects of food safety. For more information about cooking food safely, using sous vide or any other method, please consult with the FDA, USDA, or your local public health office.

Sous vide cooking safe, but it is essential to follow proper cooking temperature and time guidelines. The operations manual of your sous vide machine likely has detailed information regarding temperatures and times for different sorts of meat. There are also plenty of resources online that can provide all the information you require for cooking food safely. Also, Appendix A has Time and Temperature Charts (used with permission of Eades Appliance Technology, LLC/SousVide Supreme, www.sousvidesupreme.com), for cooking all sorts of meat in a sous vide water bath. It is important to note that this information is a guide, and there are many other factors that come into play that can impact the length it takes to properly cook and in some cases pasteurize a piece of meat. Some factors include the shape, size, and thickness of the cut of meat. Obviously, the thicker a piece of meat, the longer it will take to cook and be safe to eat. In some cases, the meat may be too thick to cook and pasteurize safely and it may be necessary to cut it into smaller portions.

It is important to note that most harmful bacteria reside on the outside of the meat. This does not include poultry like chicken and turkey that can have salmonella on the inside of the meat. But, for most other meats, the inside of the meat is generally considered sterile and free of these forms of bacteria. Ground meat is a different story because any harmful bacteria would be mixed throughout all the meat. Also, a knife or meat tenderizer that pierces the meat can send bacteria into the middle core of a solid piece of meat.

Here are a few tips for cooking safely:

- Purchase the highest-quality meat from a respected butcher or supermarket.
- Take great care to prepare the meat in a sterile environment, regularly cleaning knives, tools, cutting boards, countertops, and your hands.
- Package, cook, and consume the meat as soon after purchase as possible.
- Make sure that when the meat is being stored it is in the fridge or freezer, in a proper temperature-controlled environment.
- Read and follow FDA and USDA guidelines (or your local public health office) for the proper temperature and time for cooking meat.
- Take greater care if you or someone you are cooking for is more susceptible to illness (e.g., the elderly, pregnant women, infants, others). In these cases, cooking at a higher temperature is advised.

There are some amazing resources for cooking food safely using sous vide. One of the best tools available is in fact an iPhone/iPad app made by PolyScience. This app, called Sous Vide Toolbox, allows you to input the type of meat, including its size, shape, and thickness. Then you input the planned cooking temperature and the beginning temperature of the meat (usually a fridge temperature). This app will then calculate the time it will take to cook and pasteurize the food so that it is safe for consumption. It is impressive because you can make some minor adjustments, like increasing or decreasing the temperature by one degree or two, and immediately the app will make the adjustments and show the new time it will take to cook and pasteurize the food. This app is a minimal cost and it is an invaluable tool, providing a wealth of useful information.

Chapter 4
Advanced Techniques

Sous vide opens the door to many different culinary possibilities. Some people delve into this with the desire to expand their skills in the kitchen and make fancy dinners that will amaze their guests. Other people see sous vide mainly as a convenience. The ability to submerge meat in the water bath and not fear overcooking it is extremely appealing. There are home cooks who love the "set it and forget it" mindset of sous vide and embrace the thought of life being less stressful with sous vide in the home. Both of these mindsets are accurate and that is one of the fabulous things about sous vide cooking. It is a highly versatile cooking technique that can both advance your culinary skills and make life a whole lot easier!

Innovative Methods with Sous Vide

Sous vide is a fine way to keep cooking simple, as it is a surprisingly effortless method. It is understandable that anyone who hasn't tried cooking sous vide may feel like it is overwhelming and complicated, but that could not be further from the truth. Sous vide can be quite basic, using standard foolproof techniques every time. Its ease and straightforwardness is one of the significant advantages of sous vide. But, it doesn't end there. Anyone who wants to can use sous vide to create new and advanced culinary creations. Molecular gastronomy merges food and science to redefine cooking, food presentation, and plating. Sous vide is a regularly used cooking method in molecular gastronomy and modern cuisine in general.

There are a number of tools that the modern chef uses alongside sous vide. The following is a list of a few kitchen gadgets that can expand the sous vide enthusiasts landscape.

ESSENTIAL

All these tools and others are available for purchase online through many different sources like Amazon, Williams-Sonoma, and more. There are many different brands, products, and models, so be sure to read online reviews to discover what is best and what will fit your culinary needs.

Handheld Smoker

The ability to infuse smoke into foods that have been cooked in the sous vide opens up a whole new exciting element to this culinary sphere. A handheld smoking device uses wood shavings to create smoke that passes through a tube and into a bag or other container. The smoke penetrates the food to give it a wonderful hint of smoky flavor. It is also possible to plate a finished dish and cover it with a glass serving dome. The smoke can be sent into the dome and this allows the food to sit in that smoky environment, providing an enhanced taste experience. Companies like PolyScience and 100%Chef make handheld smoking guns that are an excellent addition to any foodie's arsenal.

Here are a few recipes found in this book that work very well with handheld smokers:

- *Chicken with Tomato Pineapple Chutney* (Chapter 8)
- *Salmon with Sun-Dried Tomato Basil Compound Butter* (Chapter 11)
- *No-Fuss Scallops* (Chapter 11)
- *Spicy Butternut Squash Soup* (Chapter 7)

Simply cook each of these recipes according to the written directions. Then, just prior to serving, place the food in a serving bowl or on a plate and cover with plastic wrap. Stick the smoking gun's tube under the plastic wrap and fill it with smoke. Let the smoke rest with the food for a couple of minutes and then serve.

Soda Siphons and Gourmet Whips

Usually, people think of soda siphons or gourmet whips as a way to make seltzer or whipped cream, but this kitchen gadget can do so much more. The gourmet whip has become an essential tool for modern cuisine and is used to make fancy foams, froths, creams, sauces, and even soup. These gourmet whips can be clamped on to the side of a sous vide water bath, allowing the ingredients inside the stainless steel canister to gently cook or simmer. This is excellent for egg-based sauces like hollandaise or anglaise. The iSi Gourmet Whip is an excellent product and a welcome addition to any foodie's kitchen tool chest.

Here are a couple of recipes that can utilize the gourmet whip with great results:

- *Pumpkin and Apple Soup* (Chapter 7)
- *Hollandaise Sauce* (Chapter 5)
- *Crème Anglaise* (Chapter 14)

Molecular Gastronomy Chemicals

Chemistry is an important aspect of molecular gastronomy. Adding specific food additives or chemicals can produce amazing results. Small amounts of agar, calcium lactate, sodium alginate, soy lecithin, tapioca maltodextrin, and others can change the look and taste of food. With these ingredients home cooks can make foams, gel spheres, films, and emulsions out of food that one never thought possible.

These additives can really help the sous vide home cook create sauces that stay syrupy, emulsifications that do not separate, and vinaigrettes that have the perfect consistency. Molecule-R is a company that makes an excellent starter pack for molecular gastronomy. The packets are portion sized and perfect for someone wanting to give this form of cooking a test run.

Making Life Simpler Sous Vide Style

The hectic pace of life can sometimes cause stress when you think about mealtime. Families can struggle balancing multiple schedules, tasks, chores, work, school, and extracurricular activities, so that even the idea of cooking dinner can bring about weariness. People often look for ways to make the actual preparation for supper simpler. Sous vide cooking definitely provides options for anyone who is strained for time, as there is an element of "set it and forget it" that comes with sous vide cooking.

Reheating Previously Cooked Food

Not only is sous vide an excellent way to cook meat, vegetables, and other foods, but it is also a great way to reheat food that was previously cooked. Food that has already gone through the process of being vacuum sealed and cooked in the sous vide is perfectly safe to be reheated at a later date. Simply leave the food in the bag, chill the food immediately after it is removed from the sous vide water bath, and place it in the fridge or freezer. Vacuum-sealed cooked meat should be good in the fridge for a day or two, while frozen meat will be good for weeks or possibly months.

ESSENTIAL

> If you are cooking food sous vide to eat on a different date, make sure to place the bag of food in an ice bath immediately after it comes out of the sous vide water bath. Let the bag chill in the ice bath to bring the temperature down rapidly and after that, it can be placed in the fridge or freezer, ready to go for a future sous vide reheat session.

To reheat food, simply set the sous vide machine to the desired serving temperature. Place the bagged, precooked food into the water bath and after about 45–60 minutes it should be reheated and ready to serve. Obviously the time to reheat would vary based on the thickness of the food in the bag, with thicker food taking a bit longer. It is not recommended to reheat thick cuts of meat, because the cooking, chilling, and cooking of larger pieces of meat creates too many opportunities for food spoilage and the growth of bacteria.

It is also possible to use sous vide as a way to reheat food that was previously cooked using other methods. In these cases, food cooked on the stovetop, in the oven, on the grill, or even outside in a smoker can be vacuum sealed and frozen. Then, at a later date, this food can be reheated in the sous vide water bath. One great example is a smoked pork shoulder that was slowly cooked in a backyard wood smoker. After cooking the pork in the smoker, it can be shredded, chilled, spread evenly into a food-safe bag, and vacuum sealed. At this point it can be thrown in the freezer. To reheat, simply heat up the sous vide water bath and submerge the bag of pulled pork in the water bath and cook until heated through, about 45–60 minutes. Using this method prevents the meat from drying out and burning in a way that could happen in the oven or stovetop.

QUESTION

Can I reheat frozen leftovers cooked another way?

Yes! The leftovers could have been cooked in the oven, stovetop, or on the grill. It does not matter at all. Simply toss the leftovers into a food-safe bag, flatten it to an even thickness of about 1 inch or less, and vacuum seal it. Then, once frozen, it can be reheated at a later date in the sous vide water bath.

This method of reheating cooked meals can be used for many different dishes. One idea is to make a big batch of food and then divide it into individual portion-sized vacuum-sealed bags. This is an excellent way for college students to get Mom's famous meals, stacked in the freezer and ready to be reheated in the sous vide.

Using Sous Vide with Other Cooking Techniques

People regularly use multiple cooking methods when making dinner. They may not realize it, and in some cases it is second nature, but switching from one cooking technique to another is fairly common. Take braised short ribs as an example. The ribs are first seared on the stovetop and then finished in the oven: two methods, one dish.

While sous vide does an excellent job cooking meat so that it is tender and juicy, it does have some limitations. It does not have the ability to brown or crisp food, which is why additional steps are recommended to finish meat and some other foods. One of the best ways to use sous vide is to incorporate its cooking strengths during meal prep alongside other cooking procedures that have different strengths.

Here are a few recipe examples found in this cookbook that use sous vide along with other cooking methods:

- *Double-Seared Beef Tenderloin* (Chapter 9) is seared in a skillet and then cooked in the sous vide. Once it comes out of the water bath it is seared again. Sous vide allows the beef to be perfectly cooked throughout while the searing creates a Maillard reaction that cannot be replicated in the water bath.
- *Buffalo Chicken Wings* (Chapter 6) are first cooked in the sous vide and then deep-fried. The water bath cooks the chicken wings so that they are moist and juicy, while the deep fryer crisps up that skin like everyone loves!
- *Pulled Pork Shepherd's Pie* (Chapter 10) is started in the sous vide with the pork being cooked in the water bath. After the meat is shredded, the shepherd's pie is assembled and then it is all baked in the oven. Now, while the sous vide is amazing for creating super-tender pork meat, it obviously could not be used as a substitute for oven baking.

Do not think that entering into the world of sous vide cooking means that everything now needs to be done in a bag and under water. Instead, the best way to use sous vide is to maximize its cooking potential and to use it where it shines.

Converting Traditional Recipes for Sous Vide

Now, while home cooks today may not keep their favorite recipes stored away in a handwritten recipe book, there is no question that people still have their "keeper" recipes. They may be in an e-mail document, posted on their Facebook timeline, or found on a popular food blog. Either way, everyone has those "tried and true" recipes that regularly make the dinner rotation.

ESSENTIAL

> Some of the most important tools in converting recipes for sous vide are the _Time and Temperature Charts_, found in Appendix A. These charts show the cooking temperature for meats, veggies, and more, as well as provide minimum and maximum cooking times. Use these guides as a starting point in making changes to those favorite recipes.

Is it possible to take these non–sous vide recipes and convert them so that they can be cooked in a water bath? Well, there is no simple answer to that. Some recipes can easily be adapted so that they can be cooked sous vide. Take oven-baked salmon with creamy dill sauce as an example. This is a delicious way to prepare salmon, and it can work just as well using sous vide. Instead of cooking the salmon in the oven, place it in a food-safe bag with any desired aromatics and vacuum seal the bag. Place it in the water bath at the temperature for salmon found in *Appendix A*. Make the dill sauce separately, and when the salmon comes out of the water bath, you will have one delicious meal.

Now, while the salmon recipe is relatively simple to convert for sous vide, others can be more challenging. Beef stew is a more complicated recipe that will require decisions to be made regarding how the recipe will be cooked. Stewing beef in the sous vide is amazing because it can be fork tender, with all the collagen dissolved, but still be medium-rare. This is something that cannot be replicated any other way. But cooking stewing beef this way will not result in tender potatoes or carrots for stew. Instead, they need to be cooked using a different method. So, to convert this recipe, maybe the best thing to do would be to cook the beef in the sous vide with a rich marinade or spice blend and then cook the rest of the stew on the stovetop, in the oven, slow cooker, or even the pressure cooker. To serve, toss the beef with the vegetables for a delicious beef stew.

There are so many options and possibilities when it comes to adapting family favorite recipes for sous vide, but there is no exact guideline. It will require some consideration for the way the food is to be cooked and what you think will work.

The Potential of Sous Vide Cooking

Just like fashion has trends that look like they will last but eventually fade away (bell bottoms anyone?), there are most definitely short-term culinary crazes. Many people have tried different food fads and likely gave the Atkins diet a try, have a fondue machine in their storage closet, right next to that bread maker they never use, and they likely paid way too much money for a gourmet cupcake. While each of these was simply a flash in the pan, popular one day and forgotten the next, sous vide cooking is looking to be a revolution, changing the way people cook.

FACT

> In many ways, sous vide is creating a paradigm shift in the kitchen, where more and more people are discovering the vast benefits that come with using this cooking technique. Companies that are making sous vide machines cannot keep them in stock, as they are selling out as quickly as they are built.

In the 1970s it was slow cooker mania when the Crock-Pot entered the market. Housewives everywhere were learning the benefits of creating one-pot meals in the slow cooker. Now, while many foodies refer to the slow cooker as the easy way to destroy a good piece of meat, there is no denying that it has survived and become a commonly used kitchen appliance. Homes all over the place use the slow cooker because of its foolproof nature and the opportunity to prep it all in the morning and get it cooking on low, knowing that dinner will be ready once you get home.

Sous vide has a similar opportunity to establish itself as an excellent way to prepare food and cook succulent meat every time. Just like almost every home has a grill, there may come a day when every home has a sous vide machine. There may come a day when people crave a juicy steak, so they get the water bath going and reach for that food-safe bag. There may come a day when people never settle for dry oven-baked chicken and instead enjoy moist and juicy sous vide chicken. There may come a day when people no longer wonder how to cook a medium-rare duck breast properly because they have learned how simple it is using the sous vide cooking technique.

There is no reason for sous vide to be a fad, because everything about it screams that it should, in fact, be a revolution. Sous vide is easy to use and incredibly forgiving, considering that it is essentially impossible to overcook meat. Sous vide allows the home cook to create dishes that rival something that could be purchased at a restaurant, and it is not that hard to do. Sous vide can be used to create a wide range of food from succulent scallops to tangy pickles, or from a juicy steak to creamy vanilla anglaise. So, don't miss out on all the benefits that come with this culinary technique. Join the sous vide revolution!

Chapter 5
Breakfast

The Perfect Egg

Using the sous vide water bath is a simple, foolproof way to cook eggs in the shell. Whether poached, soft-boiled, or hard-boiled, the sous vide can do it all!

Ingredients
Serves 1

1 large egg

1. Fill the water bath with water. Set your sous vide machine to the specific temperature based on the finished type of egg desired. Place the egg in the water bath and cook sous vide for 75 minutes.
2. The 144°F egg: The white is barely set and the yolk is runny. This is an ideal egg for udon or ramen noodles.
3. The 147°F egg: The white is firmer and the yolk is thick, creamy, and similar to pudding or custard. This egg is great for toast, hash, or eggs Benedict.
4. The 165°F egg: This is your standard hard-boiled egg. The white is hard but not rubbery and the yolk is fully set and crumbly. This egg is ideal for egg salad, deviled eggs, and potato salad.

Sweet Potato and Pork Belly Hash

With fried pork belly, sweet potato, and the perfect sous vide egg, this might just be the ultimate hash. There are a lot of steps, but it is so worth the work! For a more traditional hash you can substitute the sweet potatoes with white or yellow potatoes.

Ingredients
Serves 4

2 medium sweet potatoes
4 large eggs

½ pound <u>24-Hour Sous Vide Pork Belly</u>, diced (see recipe in Chapter 10)
1 medium yellow onion, diced
1 medium green bell pepper, cored and diced
1 teaspoon sea salt

½ teaspoon freshly ground black pepper
2 tablespoons minced fresh flat-leaf parsley

Make-Ahead Options

Since there are three different things in this recipe that use the sous vide machine (sweet potato, pork belly, and eggs), it is possible to make both the sweet potatoes and the pork belly ahead. Cool the prepared ingredients in covered containers in the refrigerator until ready to use. That makes the actual assembly of the hash in the morning quite simple.

---

1. Peel the sweet potatoes and cut them into ½" cubes.
2. Fill the water bath with water. Set your sous vide machine temperature to 183°F.

3. Place the sweet potatoes in a food-safe bag and vacuum seal the bag. Make sure the cubes of sweet potatoes are in a single layer and not stacked.
4. Place the sweet potatoes in the water bath and cook sous vide for 1½ hours. Cool in the fridge until ready to use.
5. For the eggs, set the sous vide machine to 147°F. Slowly drop the eggs into the water bath and cook sous vide for 75 minutes.
6. In a large skillet over medium heat, fry the pork belly, onion, and green pepper for about 5 minutes or until the pork belly starts to crisp and the onion and pepper are tender.
7. Stir in the sweet potatoes and continue to fry for another 7–9 minutes or until they start to become crispy. Add the salt, pepper, and parsley.
8. To serve, spoon some hash on a plate and crack an egg on top.

Hollandaise Sauce

Usually thought to be challenging to make, this sauce is super easy to make in the sous vide and just as delicious as when it's made on the stovetop.

Ingredients
Makes 1 cup

4 large egg yolks

½ cup butter, melted

1 teaspoon lemon juice

½ teaspoon sea salt

1. Whisk together all the ingredients (except the citric acid) in a small bowl.
2. Fill the water bath with water. Set your sous vide machine temperature to 150°F.
3. Pour the mixture into a food-safe zip-top bag. Slowly lower the bag into the water using the water displacement method; the air will escape from the bag. Continue to lower the bag until it is about 1" from being fully submerged. Once the bag has been lowered, zip it shut with your fingers.
4. Place the bag in the water bath and cook sous vide for 60 minutes.
5. Pour the mixture into a blender and blend until smooth and emulsified.

Eggs Benedict

Quick and easy to make, this indulgent dish is perfect for a weekend breakfast or brunch.

Ingredients
Serves 4

4 large eggs
2 English muffins, split
4 slices ham or Canadian bacon
Hollandaise Sauce (see recipe in this chapter)

1. Fill the water bath with water. Set your sous vide machine temperature to 147°F.
2. Place the eggs in the water bath and cook sous vide for 75 minutes.
3. Toast the English muffins.
4. To assemble, spoon a little Hollandaise Sauce on all 4 toasted muffin slices and top with a slice of ham. Gently crack an egg on top and spoon some more Hollandaise Sauce over the egg.

Eggs Florentine

A variation of eggs Benedict, this recipe uses sautéed spinach instead of ham.

Ingredients
Serves 4

4 large eggs
1 tablespoon butter
2 cups fresh spinach
2 English muffins, split
Hollandaise Sauce (see recipe in this chapter)

Add a Little Salmon

Lift this recipe to another level by adding a thin slice of smoked salmon. The smokiness of the salmon perfectly complements the spinach and the egg.

1. Fill the water bath with water. Set your sous vide machine temperature to 147°F.
2. Place the eggs in the water bath and cook sous vide for 75 minutes.
3. Melt the butter in a large skillet over medium heat. Add the spinach and cook until wilted, stirring often. Remove from heat.
4. Toast the English muffins.
5. To assemble, spoon a little Hollandaise Sauce on all 4 toasted muffin slices and top with some cooked spinach. Gently crack an egg on top and spoon some more Hollandaise Sauce over the egg.

Scrambled Eggs

Sous vide is quite possibly the greatest way to cook scrambled eggs. There is no need to hover over the skillet stirring; instead, just stick them in the water bath and they come out light, fluffy, and delicious.

Ingredients
Serves 2

4 large eggs

1½ tablespoons butter, melted

2 tablespoons heavy cream

⅛ teaspoon sea salt

⅛ teaspoon freshly ground black pepper

> **Double Up!**
>
> The recipe can easily be doubled and, if the water bath is large enough, you could prepare multiple batches at once. Each batch needs to be in a separate bag. This is an ideal way to make lots of scrambled eggs for a family holiday brunch.

1. Fill the water bath with water. Set your sous vide machine temperature to 167°F.
2. Place the eggs, butter, and cream in a small bowl and mix thoroughly with a whisk or immersion blender.
3. Pour the mixture into a food-safe zip-top bag. Slowly lower the bag into the water using the water displacement method; the air will escape from the bag. Continue to lower the bag until it is

about 1" from being fully submerged. Once the bag has been lowered, zip it shut with your fingers.
4. Place the eggs in the water bath and cook sous vide for 20–25 minutes. Every 5 minutes, take the bag out of the water and massage it in your hands. Use a towel to protect your hands from the heat.
5. Spoon the eggs onto 2 plates and sprinkle with salt and pepper. Serve immediately.

Asparagus and Prosciutto Scrambled Eggs

Featuring perfectly cooked, tender asparagus with light and fluffy eggs, this light breakfast showcases the wonderful results of sous vide cooking.

Ingredients
Serves 2

12 asparagus spears
1 teaspoon olive oil
4 large eggs

1½ tablespoons butter, melted
2 tablespoons heavy cream
2 slices prosciutto
2 tablespoons grated Parmesan cheese
2 tablespoons minced fresh flat-leaf parsley

⅛ teaspoon sea salt

⅛ teaspoon freshly ground black pepper

1. Trim the asparagus by snapping off the bottoms with your fingers.
2. Fill the water bath with water. Set your sous vide machine temperature to 180°F.
3. Place the asparagus and oil in a food-safe bag and vacuum seal the bag. Make sure the asparagus are lined up next to each other and are only 1 or 2 rows deep.
4. Place the asparagus in the water bath and cook sous vide for 12 minutes.

5. Leave the asparagus in the water bath and lower the temperature of the sous vide machine to 167°F and add enough cold water to quickly bring the water bath down to 167°F.
6. Place the eggs, butter, and cream in a small bowl and mix thoroughly with a whisk or immersion blender.
7. Pour the mixture into a food-safe zip-top bag. Slowly lower the bag into the water using the water displacement method; the air will escape from the bag. Continue to lower the bag until it is about 1" from being fully submerged. Once the bag has been lowered, zip it shut with your fingers.
8. Place the egg mixture in the water bath and cook sous vide for 20–25 minutes. Every 5 minutes, take the bag out of the water and massage it in your hands. Use a towel to protect your hands from the heat.
9. Remove the bag of asparagus from the water bath and wrap 1 prosciutto slice around 6 spears; place on a plate. Repeat with the second slice of prosciutto and 6 asparagus spears. Spoon some eggs on the asparagus. Top with Parmesan cheese and parsley. Sprinkle with salt and pepper.

Breakfast Burrito

Go Tex-Mex in the morning! These burritos feature a full breakfast all wrapped up in a soft burrito shell.

Ingredients
Serves 4

4 large eggs

1½ tablespoons butter, melted

2 tablespoons heavy cream

2 large avocados, peeled, pitted, and diced

2 medium tomatoes, diced

2 tablespoons minced fresh cilantro

1 medium jalapeño pepper, cored and minced

1 medium lime, juiced

½ pound breakfast sausages

4 (8") soft flour tortillas

⅛ teaspoon sea salt

⅛ teaspoon freshly ground black pepper

1 cup grated Cheddar cheese

Take These Burritos to Go!

Prepare the burritos, wrap them in aluminum foil, and they are an ideal breakfast treat to have on the go. Whether it is for the morning commute to work or the trip to school, these burritos are an awesome on-the-run breakfast.

1. Fill the water bath with water. Set your sous vide machine temperature to 167°F.
2. Place the eggs, butter, and cream in a small bowl and mix thoroughly with a whisk or immersion blender.
3. Pour the mixture into a food-safe zip-top bag. Slowly lower the bag into the water using the water displacement method; the air will escape from the bag. Continue to lower the bag until it is about 1" from being fully submerged. Once the bag has been lowered, zip it shut with your fingers.
4. Place the eggs in the water bath and cook sous vide for 20–25 minutes. Every 5 minutes, take the bag out of the water and massage it in your hands. Use a towel to protect your hands from the heat.
5. Make the salsa by mixing together the avocados, tomatoes, cilantro, jalapeño, and lime juice in a medium bowl. Cover with plastic wrap and place in the fridge.
6. Remove the sausage meat from the casings and cook in a large skillet over medium heat until browned and fully cooked, about 6–8 minutes. As the meat browns, use a wooden spoon to break it into small chunks.
7. Make the burritos by spooning the eggs equally into each tortilla and seasoning them with salt and pepper. Top with cooked sausage meat, salsa, and Cheddar cheese. Roll to close, and serve immediately.

Overnight Oatmeal

Have breakfast ready and waiting for you when you wake up in the morning with this simple recipe.

Ingredients
Serves 2

1 cup rolled oats
1 cup whole milk
1 cup water
2 packed tablespoons light brown sugar
2 tablespoons dried cranberries

½ teaspoon sea salt

Variations

This recipe can be modified with endless possibilities. Swap the brown sugar for maple syrup or honey, or use raisins, nuts, berries, or apples for the cranberries. Add some chocolate chips if you really want to turn this into a decadent treat!

1. Fill the water bath with water. Set your sous vide machine temperature to 160°F.
2. Place all the ingredients in a food-safe bag and vacuum seal the bag.
3. Place the oatmeal mixture in the water bath and cook sous vide for 8–10 hours.
4. Spoon the oatmeal into 2 bowls and serve. If desired, top with nuts, brown sugar, and milk.

Applesauce

Fresh and sweet, with a hint of cinnamon, this applesauce is a snap to make! If you prefer a chunkier applesauce, instead of using the food processor, simply mash the bag around in your hands.

Ingredients
Makes about 2 cups

5 medium apples (McIntosh, Gala, Golden Delicious, etc.)

⅓ packed cup light brown sugar

½ teaspoon ground cinnamon

1 teaspoon lemon juice

> **Oatmeal with Applesauce**
>
> Stir equal amounts of prepared applesauce with the *Overnight Oatmeal* (see recipe in this chapter) for a healthy breakfast and a great way to start your day.

1. Core, peel, and chop the apples.
2. Fill the water bath with water. Set your sous vide machine temperature to 180°F.
3. Place all the ingredients in a food-safe bag and vacuum seal the bag.
4. Place the apple mixture in the water bath and cook sous vide for 1½ hours.
5. Remove the bag from the water bath and let cool slightly. Pour the mixture into a food processor and purée until smooth.

Chapter 6
Appetizers

Buffalo Chicken Wings

The ultimate tailgate snack, these Buffalo wings are crispy on the outside, moist on the inside, and coated in an awesome spicy sauce.

Ingredients
Serves 4

2 pounds whole chicken wings

½ cup butter

1 cup hot sauce (add another ½ cup if you like it hot)
1 teaspoon Worcestershire sauce
1 teaspoon garlic salt
1 teaspoon freshly ground black pepper

½ cup all-purpose flour

Party Planning

Hosting a Super Bowl party or some other event and need to make lots of chicken wings? Cook all that you need in the sous vide water bath the day before and they are ready to be deep-fried the day of the event. Make more than one kind of sauce for different choices as well.

1. Cut the chicken wings into 3 pieces. Keep the drumettes and wingettes (flats), but throw away the wing tips.
2. Fill the water bath with water. Set your sous vide machine temperature to 176°F.
3. Place the chicken wing pieces in a food-safe bag and vacuum seal the bag. Make sure they are lined up side by side and not

stacked or piled. Use multiple bags if necessary.
4. Place the chicken wings in the water bath and cook sous vide for 3 hours.
5. To make the buffalo sauce, melt the butter in a medium saucepan over medium heat. Add all the remaining ingredients except the flour and simmer for about 10 minutes, stirring often.
6. Prepare a Dutch oven or deep fryer with oil; preheat oil to 350°F.
7. Remove the chicken wings from the bag and pat dry with a paper towel.
8. Dredge the wings in flour. Shake off excess flour and deep-fry the chicken in 350°F oil for about 8–10 minutes.
9. Place the wings on paper towels to remove the excess oil and then toss them with buffalo sauce.

Honey Garlic Chicken Wings

These wings are sweet and lip-smackingly delicious! Even though this recipe includes a homemade sauce, store-bought honey garlic sauces work great as well.

Ingredients
Serves 4

2 pounds whole chicken wings

1/3 cup butter

8–10 cloves garlic, minced

1/2 cup soy sauce

1 cup honey

2 teaspoons water

1 teaspoon cornstarch

1/2 cup all-purpose flour

1. Cut the chicken wings into 3 pieces. Keep the drumettes and wingettes (flats), but throw away the wing tips.
2. Fill the water bath with water. Set your sous vide machine temperature to 176°F.
3. Place the chicken wing pieces in a food-safe bag and vacuum seal the bag. Make sure they are lined up side by side and not stacked or piled. Use multiple bags if necessary.
4. Place the wings in the water bath and cook sous vide for 3 hours.
5. To make the sauce, melt the butter in a medium saucepan over medium heat. Add the minced garlic and cook for 2–3 minutes

to release the flavor.
6. Add the soy sauce and honey and bring to a boil. Lower the heat to a simmer.
7. In small bowl, whisk together the water and cornstarch to make a slurry. Whisk the slurry into the honey sauce and continue to stir as the sauce thickens over the next 3–4 minutes.
8. Prepare a Dutch oven or deep fryer with oil; preheat oil to 350°F.
9. Remove the chicken wings from the bag and pat dry with a paper towel.
10. Dredge the wings in flour. Shake off the excess flour and deep-fry the wings in 350°F oil for about 8–10 minutes.
11. Place the wings on paper towels to remove the excess oil and toss them with the honey garlic sauce.

Sous Vide Chicken Wings (for Buffalo Chicken Wings and Honey Garlic Chicken Wings)

Hummus

There is no need to buy hummus in the store when it is this easy to make and a fraction of the cost. Serve this hummus with pita bread, crackers, or veggies.

Ingredients
Serves 4–6

½ cup dried chickpeas
2 cups water, divided
2 cloves garlic, divided
1 tablespoon lemon juice
2 tablespoons tahini

½ teaspoon sea salt
2 tablespoons extra-virgin olive oil
1 teaspoon ground cumin

1. Fill the water bath with water. Set your sous vide machine temperature to 195°F.
2. Place the chickpeas, 1½ cups water, and 1 clove garlic in a large food-safe zip-top bag. Slowly lower the zip-top bag into the water and, using the water displacement method, the air will escape from the bag. Continue to lower the bag until it is about 1" from being fully submerged. Once the bag has been lowered, zip it shut with your fingers.
3. Cook sous vide for 3½ hours. Check to see if chickpeas are tender and cook longer if needed.
4. Drain the chickpeas and let them cool until they come to room temperature.

5. Using a food processor, pulse the chickpeas, lemon juice, remaining garlic clove, tahini, salt, oil, and cumin. While the food processor is running, slowly pour in the remaining water. Check the texture and thickness of the hummus. If needed, add more water to reach the desired consistency.
6. When ready to serve, scoop the hummus into a small serving bowl and serve with pita bread, crackers, or fresh vegetables.

Hummus

Baba Ghanouj

This Egyptian version of baba ghanouj is similar to hummus, but instead of chickpeas, cooked eggplant is used. Serve this with toasted baguettes, crackers, or veggies.

Ingredients
Serves 4–6

1 large eggplant, peeled and cubed
1 tablespoon lemon juice
2 cloves garlic
2 tablespoons tahini
1 teaspoon sea salt
2 tablespoons extra-virgin olive oil
2 tablespoons chopped fresh cilantro

1. Fill the water bath with water. Set your sous vide machine temperature to 185°F.
2. Place the cubed eggplant in a food-safe bag and vacuum seal the bag. Make sure the eggplant is in only 1–2 layers within the bag. Use multiple bags if necessary.
3. Place the eggplant in the water bath and cook sous vide for 2–3 hours.
4. Using a food processor, pulse the cooked eggplant, lemon juice, garlic, tahini, salt, and olive oil. Process until smooth and creamy.
5. Add the cilantro and pulse a few times or until it is evenly mixed throughout the dip. Serve.

White Bean and Artichoke Dip

This is an easy snack that is great for any party. It is delicious and healthy, without any guilt! Serve with pita bread, crackers, or veggies.

Ingredients
Serves 4–6

½ cup dried cannellini beans

1½ cups water

2 cloves garlic, divided
1 (14-ounce) can artichoke hearts, drained
2 tablespoons lemon juice
2 tablespoons extra-virgin olive oil

½ teaspoon sea salt

⅓ cup grated Parmesan cheese

1. Fill the water bath with water. Set your sous vide machine temperature to 195°F.
2. Place the beans, 1½ cups water, and 1 clove garlic in a large food-safe zip-top bag. Slowly lower the zip-top bag into the water and, using the water displacement method, the air will escape from the bag. Continue to lower the bag until it is about 1" from being fully submerged. Once the bag has been lowered, zip it shut with your fingers
3. Cook sous vide for 3½ hours. Check to see if the beans are tender and cook a little longer if needed.

4. Drain the beans and let them cool until they come to room temperature.
5. Using a food processor, pulse the beans, artichoke hearts, lemon juice, remaining garlic clove, oil, salt, and Parmesan cheese. Process until smooth and creamy. If a thinner consistency is desired, add a little extra water while processing. Serve.

Shrimp and Avocado Salsa

This salsa is both light and hearty and could almost be served as a meal all by itself! Serve this salsa chilled with tortilla chips.

Ingredients
Serves 4–6

1 pound raw medium shrimp, peeled and deveined
1 tablespoon olive oil
2 medium avocados, peeled, cored, and cubed
3 medium tomatoes, diced
2 medium jalapeño peppers, cored and minced

¼ cup chopped fresh cilantro

Juice of 2 medium limes

½ teaspoon sea salt

Shrimp in the Sous Vide

Shrimp are one of the more delicate things to cook and it is easy to overcook them, resulting in mushy shrimp with little taste. Sous vide cooking, with its degree of temperature precision, is an ideal way to cook shrimp perfectly every time.

---

1. Fill the water bath with water. Set your sous vide machine temperature to 140°F.
2. Place the shrimp and olive oil in a food-safe bag and vacuum seal the bag.
3. Place the shrimp in the water bath and cook sous vide for 30 minutes.
4. Remove the shrimp from the bag and cut each into 2–3 pieces.

5. In a large mixing bowl, combine all the ingredients and toss.
6. Let the salsa marinate, in the refrigerator, for 10–15 minutes before serving.

Shrimp and Avocado Salsa

Tomato and Mango Salsa

This fruity salsa is full of tropical flavors and is perfect served with tortilla chips on a hot summer day.

Ingredients
Serves 4–6

2 tablespoons extra-virgin olive oil
3 medium tomatoes, diced
2 large ripe mangos, peeled, pitted, and diced
1 medium red onion, diced
2 tablespoons chopped fresh cilantro
1 tablespoon minced fresh mint
Juice of 1 medium lime
1 tablespoon granulated sugar

½ teaspoon sea salt

1. Fill the water bath with water. Set your sous vide machine temperature to 150°F.
2. Place the oil, tomatoes, mangos, and red onion in a food-safe bag and vacuum seal the bag.
3. Place the bag in the water bath and cook sous vide for 1 hour. Quick chill the bag by placing it in an ice bath.
4. Empty the bag into a large bowl and toss well with the remaining ingredients. Let the salsa marinate, in the refrigerator, for 10–15 minutes before serving.

Shrimp and Jalapeño Quesadilla

Go Mexican with these bite-sized appetizers. The shrimp are perfectly cooked in the sous vide water bath and go very well with the lime, cilantro, and jalapeño kick.

Ingredients
Serves 6–8

1 pound raw medium shrimp, peeled and deveined
1 tablespoon olive oil
2 jalapeño peppers, cored and minced
3 green onions, sliced
3 tablespoons minced fresh cilantro
2 tablespoons lime juice

½ teaspoon sea salt
6–8 (8") soft flour tortillas
1 cup grated Cheddar cheese
1 cup grated Monterey jack cheese

> **Grill It!**
>
> During those warm summer months, the grill is an ideal way to cook these quesadillas. Just follow this recipe and, instead of baking them in the oven, throw them on a hot grill for about 10 minutes.

1. Fill the water bath with water. Set your sous vide machine temperature to 140°F.
2. Place the shrimp and olive oil in a food-safe bag and vacuum seal the bag.

3. Place the shrimp in the water bath and cook sous vide for 30 minutes.
4. Preheat oven to 350°F.
5. Remove the shrimp from the bag and cut each into 2–3 pieces.
6. Place the shrimp and the jalapeño, green onions, cilantro, lime juice, and salt in a large bowl and toss to combine.
7. To make the quesadillas: scoop some of the shrimp mixture onto half of a soft tortilla. Evenly sprinkle some of each cheese onto the shrimp mixture and then fold the soft tortilla over, covering the shrimp and cheese. Repeat with all the quesadillas.
8. Bake the quesadillas in the oven until the cheese melts and the tortillas are brown, about 10 minutes.
9. Cut each quesadillas into 4 wedges and serve with salsa.

Shrimp and Jalapeño Quesadilla

Deep-Fried Pork Belly Skewers with Honey Garlic Glaze

Crispy on the outside and melt-in-your-mouth tender in the middle, these pork belly skewers taste like heaven on a skewer.

Ingredients
Serves 6–8

⅓ cup butter
8 cloves garlic, minced
2 medium Thai chilies, sliced

½ cup soy sauce
1 cup honey
1 pound *24-Hour Sous Vide Pork Belly* (see recipe in Chapter 10)
12–16 small skewers
1 tablespoon vegetable oil

1. First make the glaze: melt the butter in a small saucepan over medium heat. Add the minced garlic and chilies and cook for 2–3 minutes to release the flavor. Add the soy sauce and honey and bring to a boil. Lower the heat to a simmer. The sauce will thicken after 10 minutes or so.
2. Slice the pork belly into 1" chunks. Spear the chunks onto the skewers.
3. Add the oil to a deep, heavy pan or deep fryer and heat to 325°F. Slowly place the skewered pork belly in the hot oil and cook for about 4 minutes. The outside should be crispy and golden in color.

4. Remove the pork from the oil and drain on paper towels for 1–2 minutes.
5. Place the pork on a serving plate and drizzle with the honey garlic glaze.

Deep-Fried Pork Belly Skewers with Honey Garlic Glaze

Tomato Confit and Provolone Grilled Cheese Sandwich Wedges

This is not your average grilled cheese. It is perfect for those who prefer the finer things in life.

Ingredients
Serves 4–6

2 pints cherry tomatoes

¼ cup olive oil

1½ tablespoons balsamic vinegar

½ teaspoon sea salt

½ teaspoon black pepper

¼ cup butter or margarine, softened

8 slices fresh bread

8 slices provolone or mozzarella cheese

⅓ cup thinly sliced fresh basil

1. Fill the water bath with water. Set your sous vide machine temperature to 150°F.
2. Place the tomatoes, olive oil, vinegar, sea salt, and black pepper in a food-safe bag and vacuum seal the bag.
3. Place the tomatoes in the water bath and cook sous vide for 4 hours.
4. Remove the tomatoes from the water bath and cool to room temperature. Strain the oil and peel the skins off the tomatoes.

The skins should peel off easily.
5. Butter 1 side of each slice of bread. Assemble the sandwiches by laying out a slice of bread buttered side down. Place a slice of cheese on the bread. Put some tomatoes on top of the cheese and sprinkle with fresh basil. Add another slice of cheese and finish the sandwich with another bread slice, buttered side on the outside.
6. Place the sandwiches in a large skillet over medium heat. Cook until golden brown on each side, about 4 minutes per side. Cut the sandwiches into wedges and serve.

Flank Steak, Apricot, and Brie Bites

Tender and light, these canapés can easily be made ahead and are ideal for any party.

Ingredients
Serves 6

1 flank steak (about 2 pounds)
1 teaspoon sea salt
1 teaspoon freshly ground black pepper
1 teaspoon paprika
1 medium wheel Brie
10–12 dried apricots
20–24 fresh mint leaves
Toothpicks

1. Fill the water bath with water. Set your sous vide machine temperature to 135°F.
2. Rub the flank steak all over with the salt, pepper, and paprika. Place the steak in a food-safe bag and vacuum seal the bag.
3. Place the steak in the water bath and cook sous vide for 12–18 hours.
4. Remove from the water bath and immediately place in an ice bath to chill the steak. Cut the flank steak, against the grain, into thin slices.
5. Cut the Brie cheese into small slices and cut the dried apricots in half.
6. Assemble the bites by placing a mint leaf and dried apricot half on a piece of sliced Brie. Wrap with a slice of flank steak and

pierce with a toothpick. Keep them in the fridge until ready to serve.

Pork Tenderloin, Tomato, and Bocconcini Canapés

This canapé has the amazing and classic combination of tomato, bocconcini (small mozzarella balls), and basil, but adds a slice of super-tender pork tenderloin. The result is one outstanding bite-sized appetizer that is perfect for game day, but also fancy enough for a dinner party.

Ingredients
Serves 4

½ teaspoon sea salt

½ teaspoon freshly ground black pepper

1 pork tenderloin (about 1 pound)

1 tablespoon oil with a high smoke point (like peanut, sunflower, corn, vegetable, or safflower oil)

1 baguette, sliced and lightly toasted

3–4 plum or Roma tomatoes, sliced

1 (8-ounce) container bocconcini, drained and sliced

1 bunch fresh basil

2 tablespoons balsamic vinegar (optional)

Making Changes

There are so many ways to change up this recipe for a unique twist. Instead of fresh tomato slices, some other options include roasted red pepper, cucumber, or sun-dried tomato. Brie, Cheddar, and even goat cheese are great options to replace the bocconcini. Spread a little bit of pesto or black olive tapenade on the baguette for some added richness as well!

1. Rub the salt and pepper all over the tenderloin.
2. Fill the water bath with water. Set your sous vide machine temperature to 140°F.
3. Place the pork tenderloin in a food-safe bag and vacuum seal the bag.
4. Place the pork in the water bath and cook sous vide for 3 hours.
5. Remove the pork tenderloin from the bag and pat dry with a paper towel.
6. Heat the oil in a large skillet over high heat. Sear the tenderloin in the skillet for 45–60 seconds per side. Slice the pork into ½" medallions.
7. Assemble the canapés by layering each baguette slice with a slice of pork tenderloin, tomato, bocconcini, and a fresh basil leaf. If desired, drizzle with a little balsamic vinegar.

Pork Tenderloin, Tomato, and Bocconcini Canapés

Chapter 7
Soups and Salads

Potato and Green Bean Salad with Honey Lemon Vinaigrette

The sweet tang of the dressing brings a unique twist to potato salad.

Ingredients
Serves 4–6

2 pounds baby potatoes, quartered
1 pound green beans, trimmed
6 green onions, thinly sliced

⅓ cup extra-virgin olive oil

3 tablespoons fresh lemon juice
3 tablespoons honey

½ teaspoon sea salt

½ teaspoon freshly ground black pepper

1. Fill the water bath with water. Set your sous vide machine temperature to 183°F.
2. Place the quartered potatoes in a food-safe bag and vacuum seal the bag.
3. Place the green beans in a food-safe bag and vacuum seal the bag.
4. Place the potatoes in the water bath and cook sous vide for 30 minutes. Add the bag of green beans to the bath, with the potatoes still in the bath, and cook for 1 hour more.
5. Remove the vegetables from the water bath and place them in an ice-water bath to quickly chill them.

6. Drain the potatoes and place in a large bowl. Drain the green beans, cut in half, and place in the bowl. Add the green onions to the bowl.
7. Make the vinaigrette by whisking together the oil, lemon juice, honey, salt, and black pepper in a small bowl.
8. Pour the vinaigrette over the salad and stir until everything is coated.
9. Place in the fridge until ready to serve.

Bacon and Egg Potato Salad

This recipe uses sous vide cooking techniques to make classic potato salad. Bring this on your next picnic or to a family reunion and get rave reviews!

Ingredients
Serves 4–6

2 pounds baby potatoes, quartered
1 pound bacon
4 stalks celery, thinly sliced
4 green onions, thinly sliced
4 large hard-boiled eggs, sliced
1 cup mayonnaise
3 tablespoons white vinegar
2 teaspoons Worcestershire sauce
2 teaspoons hot sauce
2 teaspoons granulated sugar

½ teaspoon sea salt

½ teaspoon freshly ground black pepper

Potatoes That Do Not Crumble

Cooking vegetables in the sous vide has the benefit that they do not overcook. For potato salad, this is excellent as the pieces of potato do not get mushy or crumble when stirred with the rest of the salad and dressing.

---

1. Fill the water bath with water. Set your sous vide machine temperature to 183°F.

2. Place the quartered potatoes in a food-safe bag and vacuum seal the bag.
3. Place the potatoes in the water bath and cook sous vide for 1½ hours.
4. Remove the potatoes from the water bath and place them in an ice-water bath to quickly chill them.
5. Brown the bacon in a large skillet over medium-high heat. Drain on a paper towel, crumble, and set aside.
6. Drain the potatoes and place in a large bowl. Add the bacon, celery, green onions, and eggs to the bowl.
7. Make the dressing by whisking together the remaining ingredients until smooth and creamy.
8. Pour the dressing over the salad and stir until everything is coated.
9. Place in the fridge until ready to serve.

Bean Salad

While bean salads have been a staple at potlucks and picnics for decades, this recipe brings a freshness to this classic salad.

Ingredients
Serves 4–6

1 pound green beans, trimmed
2 cups cooked kidney beans
2 cups cooked chickpeas
1 medium sweet onion, diced
1 medium red bell pepper, cored and diced

½ cup extra-virgin olive oil

½ cup white vinegar

½ cup granulated sugar

1 teaspoon sea salt

½ teaspoon black pepper

1 tablespoon minced fresh flat-leaf parsley

1. Fill the water bath with water. Set your sous vide machine temperature to 183°F.
2. Place the green beans in a food-safe bag and vacuum seal the bag.
3. Place the bag in the water bath and cook sous vide for 1 hour.
4. Remove the green beans from the water bath and place in an ice-water bath to quickly chill them.
5. Drain the green beans, cut in half, and place in a large bowl. Add the kidney beans, chickpeas, onion, and bell pepper.

6. Make the vinaigrette by whisking together the oil, vinegar, sugar, salt, black pepper, and parsley in a small bowl.
7. Pour the vinaigrette over the salad and stir until everything is coated.
8. Place in the fridge until ready to serve.

Flank Steak, Mandarin Orange, and Spinach Salad

This perfectly cooked medium-rare flank steak is tender, delicious, and goes great with the oranges in this salad.

Ingredients
Serves 4–6

1 flank steak (about 2 pounds)
1 teaspoon sea salt, divided
1 teaspoon freshly ground black pepper, divided

½ cup slivered almonds

¼ cup plus 3 tablespoons granulated sugar, divided

⅓ cup extra-virgin olive oil

¼ cup white vinegar

2 tablespoons fresh flat-leaf parsley
4 cups baby spinach

⅔ cup thinly sliced celery

½ cup thinly sliced green onions

1 (11-ounce) can mandarin oranges, drained
1 tablespoon oil with a high smoke point (like peanut, sunflower, corn, vegetable, or safflower oil)

1. Fill the water bath with water. Set your sous vide machine temperature to 135°F.

2. Rub the flank steak all over with ½ teaspoon salt and ½ teaspoon pepper. Place the steak in a food-safe bag and vacuum seal the bag.
3. Place the steak in the water bath and cook sous vide for 12–18 hours.
4. Prepare the candied almonds by cooking the almonds and 3 tablespoons sugar in a medium skillet over medium heat. Stir the almonds constantly. Once the sugar is melted and the almonds are toasted, remove the pan from the heat. Pour the almonds on a sheet of aluminum foil and spread out. Allow the sugar and almonds to cool completely and then break apart into small chunks.
5. Make the vinaigrette by whisking together the ¼ cup sugar, oil, vinegar, ½ teaspoon salt, and ½ teaspoon black pepper in a small bowl.
6. In a large serving bowl, toss the parsley, baby spinach, celery, green onions, mandarin oranges, and almonds with the vinaigrette.
7. Remove the steak from the bag and pat dry with a paper towel.
8. Heat the oil in a large skillet on high heat. Sear the steak in the skillet for about 45–60 seconds per side.
9. Cut the flank steak against the grain into thin slices and place on top of the salad. Serve.

Chicken and Caesar Salad

Sous vide chicken is tender, moist, and will likely amaze anyone trying this Caesar salad. Chicken breast has never been cooked so perfectly!

Ingredients
Serves 4

2 (4-ounce) boneless, skinless chicken breasts

½ teaspoon sea salt

½ teaspoon freshly ground black pepper

1 large head romaine lettuce, roughly chopped

1 cup croutons

⅓ cup bacon bits

¾ cup Caesar salad dressing

1 tablespoon oil with a high smoke point (like peanut, sunflower, corn, vegetable, or safflower oil)

¼ cup grated Parmesan cheese

1. Fill the water bath with water. Set your sous vide machine temperature to 146°F.
2. Rub the chicken breasts all over with the salt and pepper. Place the chicken in a food-safe bag and vacuum seal the bag.
3. Place the chicken in the water bath and cook sous vide for 1½ to 4 hours.
4. In a large serving bowl, toss the romaine lettuce, croutons, and bacon bits with the salad dressing.

5. Remove the chicken from the bag and pat dry with a paper towel.
6. Heat the oil in a large skillet on high heat. Sear the chicken for about 45–60 seconds per side.
7. Cut the chicken against the grain into thin slices and place on top of the salad.
8. Sprinkle with Parmesan cheese and serve.

Duck Breast and Arugula Salad with Blueberry Vinaigrette

This salad is full of bold flavors that come together to make something incredible! The duck breast is both moist and tender with crispy skin.

Ingredients
Serves 4

- 2 (6–8-ounce) boneless duck breasts, skin on
- ½ teaspoon sea salt
- ½ teaspoon freshly ground black pepper
- 4 cups arugula leaves
- 2 medium apples (Royal Gala, Red Delicious, etc.), cored and sliced
- ¾ cup soft goat cheese, crumbled
- ½ cup toasted pine nuts
- ⅔ cup *Blueberry Vinaigrette* (see recipe in this chapter)
- 1 tablespoon oil with a high smoke point (like peanut, sunflower, corn, vegetable, or safflower oil)

> **Make It Right on the Plate!**
>
> For a fancier plating idea, try assembling the salad on 4 individual salad plates. Start by placing 1 cup of arugula leaves on the plate. Lay out some apple slices and duck breast on top. Sprinkle on the goat cheese and pine nuts and drizzle with vinaigrette.

1. Fill the water bath with water. Set your sous vide machine temperature to 135°F.
2. Rub the duck breasts all over with the salt and pepper. Place the duck in a food-safe bag and vacuum seal the bag.
3. Place the duck in the water bath and cook sous vide for 90 minutes.
4. In a large serving bowl, toss the arugula, sliced apples, goat cheese, and pine nuts with the vinaigrette.
5. Remove the duck from the bag and pat dry with a paper towel.
6. Heat the oil in a large skillet on medium heat. Sear the duck, skin side down, over medium heat for about 3–4 minutes. The skin should be crispy and the fat rendered.
7. Cut the duck breast against the grain into thin slices and place on top of the salad.

Blueberry Vinaigrette

This salad dressing is excellent with any mixed green salad.

Ingredients
Makes about 1 cup

1 pint fresh blueberries
1 teaspoon granulated sugar

⅓ cup extra-virgin olive oil

⅓ cup grape seed oil

3 tablespoons white wine vinegar
1 tablespoon balsamic vinegar
1 tablespoon Dijon mustard

Swap the Berries!

To modify this recipe simply follow the instructions, but use different berries in place of the blueberries. Some berries that work really well with this recipe include raspberries or strawberries.

1. Fill the water bath with water. Set your sous vide machine temperature to 150°F.
2. Place the blueberries in a food-safe bag and vacuum seal the bag. Make sure the blueberries are in 1 layer in the bag and not stacked.
3. Place the blueberries in the water bath and cook sous vide for 30–40 minutes.
4. Remove from the water bath and cool to room temperature.
5. Using an immersion blender, upright blender, or food processor blend all the ingredients together. Blend until smooth and

emulsified.
6. Keep in the fridge until needed.

Blueberry Vinaigrette

Spicy Butternut Squash Soup

This creamy soup is infused with Thai spices and is perfect for a light lunch or to start off a nice dinner.

Ingredients
Serves 4

4 cups cubed butternut squash (1" cubes)
2 medium Thai chilies, minced
2 tablespoons butter
1 medium onion, diced
2 cloves garlic, minced
2 cups chicken broth

¾ cup canned coconut milk

½ teaspoon sea salt

½ teaspoon freshly ground black pepper

1. Fill the water bath with water. Set your sous vide machine temperature to 183°F.
2. Place the butternut squash and the chilies in a food-safe bag and vacuum seal the bag.
3. Place the bag in the water bath and cook sous vide for 1½ hours.
4. In a medium skillet or saucepan, melt the butter over medium heat and sauté the onion and garlic until transparent and starting to caramelize, about 10 minutes.
5. Remove the squash from the water bath and pour into a blender. Add the cooked onion and remaining ingredients to the

blender.
6. Blend on high until smooth. If a thinner soup is desired, add a little more water or chicken broth. This soup can be served hot or chilled.

Spicy Butternut Squash Soup

Pumpkin and Apple Soup

This soup is smooth, fruity, and ideal for those cool autumn days.

Ingredients
Serves 4

3 cups cubed fresh pumpkin (1" cubes)

2 medium apples, (McIntosh, Gala, or other) peeled, cored, and diced

2 tablespoons butter

1 medium sweet onion, diced

2 cloves garlic, minced

3½ cups chicken broth

½ teaspoon sea salt

½ teaspoon freshly ground black pepper

⅓ cup chopped cashews

1. Fill the water bath with water. Set your sous vide machine temperature to 183°F.
2. Place the pumpkin and apples in a food-safe bag and vacuum seal the bag.
3. Place the bag in the water bath and cook sous vide for 1½ hours.
4. In a medium skillet or saucepan, melt the butter over medium heat and sauté the onion and garlic until transparent and starting to caramelize, about 10 minutes.
5. Remove the pumpkin and apples from the water bath and pour into a blender. Add the cooked onion and garlic, the chicken

broth, salt, and pepper to the blender.
6. Blend on high until smooth. If a thinner soup is desired, add a little more water or chicken broth.
7. To serve, heat the soup, ladle into soup bowls, and top with chopped cashews.

Pork Belly and Udon Noodle Soup

This soup is a Japanese classic and is full of hearty flavors and healthy ingredients.

Ingredients
Serves 4

- 4 large eggs (optional)
- 1 pound <u>24-Hour Sous Vide Pork Belly</u>, diced (see recipe in Chapter 10)
- 4 cups <u>Dashi Stock</u> (see recipe in this chapter), or chicken or vegetable broth
- 1 clove garlic
- 1" piece gingerroot, peeled
- 2 tablespoons soybean paste
- 1 cup sliced baby bok choy
- 1 cup shimeji mushrooms
- 1 (12–16-ounce) package udon noodles, cooked
- Soy sauce, to taste (optional)
- Sriracha sauce, to taste (optional)

1. Fill the water bath with water. Set your sous vide machine temperature to 144°F. Place the eggs in the water bags and cook for 75 minutes.
2. Preheat oven to 325°F.
3. Cut the pork belly into 4 equal portions. Place the pork skin side down in an ovenproof skillet and cook over medium heat for about 5 minutes, or until the skin starts to crisp. Place the skillet in the oven and cook for about 20 minutes, or until

heated throughout. Remove from the oven and cut the pork belly into ¼" slices.
4. In a large pot, heat the stock, garlic, and ginger over medium heat. Whisk in the soybean paste until dissolved. Bring to a boil and add the bok choy, mushrooms, and cooked noodles.
5. Ladle some soup into a serving bowl. Place some pork belly slices on the soup. Crack an egg on top, if desired. Add some soy sauce and sriracha sauce, if desired.

Pork Belly and Udon Noodle Soup

Dashi Stock

This broth is a base for many different Japanese soups including the Pork Belly and Udon Noodle Soup recipe found in this chapter.

Ingredients
Makes 4 cups

4 cups water
1 kombu sheet (about 4" × 5" in size)
1 dried shiitake mushroom

1. Fill the water bath with water. Set your sous vide machine temperature to 195°F.
2. Place all the ingredients in a large mason jar and hand-tighten the lid.
3. Lower the jar in the water bath and make sure that the water in the bath comes up to the lid of the jar. Cook sous vide for 1 hour.
4. Remove the jar from the water bath and strain the stock with a fine sieve. The stock is ready to be used in soup. It can also be chilled and placed in the fridge for two days.

Chapter 8
Chicken

The Ultimate Chicken Breast

Never have a tough and dried-out chicken breast again! Cooking chicken breast in a sous vide water bath results in moist and tender meat every time. You can slice this chicken and put it in a salad or wrap, or use it as a pizza topping.

Ingredients
Serves 1

1 (4-ounce) boneless, skinless chicken breast

½ teaspoon sea salt

½ teaspoon freshly ground black pepper

1 tablespoon oil with a high smoke point (like peanut, sunflower, corn, vegetable, or safflower oil), optional

Minimum and Maximum Time

Cooking in a sous vide water bath is extremely forgiving and does not require you to pull out the meat once it is fully cooked. With the case of a boneless, skinless chicken breast, it is fully cooked after $1\frac{1}{2}$ hours, but it can stay in the water bath for 4 hours, without any negative impact on the taste of the chicken.

1. Sprinkle the chicken breast with the salt and pepper. Place the chicken breast in a food-safe bag and vacuum seal it.
2. Fill the water bath with water. Set your sous vide machine temperature to 146°F.
3. Place the chicken in the water bath and cook sous vide for 1½–4 hours.

4. Take the chicken out of the water bath and pat dry with a paper towel. If desired, sear the chicken in a skillet, with oil, on high heat for about 30–45 seconds per side.

Rosemary Chicken with Cognac Mushroom Cream Sauce

The sous vide water bath infuses the chicken breast with the flavor of fresh rosemary that is perfectly paired with this decadent cream sauce.

Ingredients
Serves 4

1½ teaspoons sea salt, divided

1 teaspoon freshly ground black pepper

4 (4-ounce) boneless, skinless chicken breasts

7 tablespoons butter, divided

4 sprigs rosemary

2 cups quartered cremini mushrooms

¼ cup cognac

1½ cups heavy cream

1 tablespoon oil with a high smoke point (like peanut, sunflower, corn, vegetable, or safflower oil), optional

1. Sprinkle 1 teaspoon of the salt and the pepper on the chicken breasts. Place the chicken breasts, 4 tablespoons of the butter, and the rosemary sprigs in a food-safe bag and vacuum seal it. Make sure the chicken is lined up side by side and not stacked or piled. Use multiple bags if necessary.
2. Fill the water bath with water. Set your sous vide machine temperature to 146°F.

3. Place the chicken in the water bath and cook sous vide for 1½–4 hours.
4. Make the cognac mushroom cream sauce by melting the remaining 3 tablespoons butter in a medium saucepan over medium-high heat. Add the mushrooms and sauté, stirring often, until tender and starting to brown. Add the cognac and let it bubble and boil off for about 1 minute. Stir in the cream, lower the heat, and let simmer for about 10 minutes. Stir in the remaining ½ teaspoon salt.
5. Take the chicken out of the water bath and pat dry with a paper towel. If desired, sear the chicken in a large skillet, with oil, on high heat for about 30–45 seconds per side.
6. To serve, place the chicken breasts on dinner plates and pour some of the cognac mushroom cream sauce over the chicken.

Rosemary Chicken with Cognac Mushroom Cream Sauce

Chicken with Tomato Pineapple Chutney

A simple recipe with bright flavors that is light, healthy, and delicious. The chutney can be made days ahead and stored in the fridge until the chicken is cooked.

Ingredients
Serves 4

- 4 (4-ounce) boneless, skinless chicken breasts
- 1 teaspoon sea salt
- 1 teaspoon freshly ground black pepper
- 2 cups *Tomato Pineapple Chutney* (see recipe in Chapter 15)
- 1 tablespoon oil with a high smoke point (like peanut, sunflower, corn, vegetable, or safflower oil), optional
- ¼ cup minced fresh mint

> **With the Skin On?**
>
> It is definitely possible to cook the chicken breast with the skin on and the temperature and cooking time remain the same. Some feel that chicken cooked with the skin on comes out moister. Simply peel off the skin and use the chicken in any recipe as you normally would. For a more pleasant plating appearance, it is possible to crisp up the skin. Heat 1 tablespoon of oil in a skillet on medium heat. Lay the chicken skin side down and let it sear for a few minutes, and the skin will crisp right up.

1. Sprinkle the chicken breasts with the salt and pepper. Place the chicken breasts in a food-safe bag and vacuum seal it. Make sure the chicken is lined up side by side and not stacked or piled. Use multiple bags if necessary.

2. Fill the water bath with water. Set your sous vide machine temperature to 146°F.
3. Place the chicken in the water bath and cook sous vide for 1½–4 hours.
4. If you prefer the chutney to be warm when served, about 30 minutes before the chicken is finished cooking, place the chutney in a large food-safe zipper bag.
5. Slowly lower the bag into the water using the water displacement method, and the air will escape from the bag. Continue to lower the bag until it is about 1" from being fully submerged. Once the bag has been lowered just zip it shut with your fingers.
6. Take the chicken out of the water bath and pat dry with a paper towel. If desired, sear the chicken in a large skillet, with oil, on high heat for about 30–45 seconds per side.
7. To serve, place the chicken breasts on dinner plates, spoon some of the Tomato Pineapple Chutney over the chicken, and sprinkle some fresh mint on top.

Chicken with Bruschetta and Basil

The sweetness of the tomatoes and basil, the zip of the lemon juice, and the saltiness of the feta all combine for an excellent topping to go with chicken.

Ingredients
Serves 4

4 (4-ounce) boneless, skinless chicken breasts
1 teaspoon sea salt
1 teaspoon freshly ground black pepper
5 medium plum or Roma tomatoes, diced

¼ medium sweet onion, minced

2 cloves garlic, minced

¼ cup extra-virgin olive oil
2 tablespoons lemon juice
1 cup crumbled feta cheese

¼ cup torn fresh basil

1. Sprinkle the chicken breasts with the salt and pepper. Place the chicken breasts in a food-safe bag and vacuum seal it. Make sure the chicken is lined up side by side and not stacked or piled. Use multiple bags if necessary.
2. Fill the water bath with water. Set your sous vide machine temperature to 146°F.
3. Place the chicken in the water bath and cook sous vide for 1½–4 hours.

4. Make the bruschetta by mixing together the tomatoes, onion, garlic, olive oil, lemon juice, and crumbled feta in a medium bowl. Set aside.
5. Set oven to broil.
6. Take the chicken out of the water bath and pat dry with a paper towel. Place the chicken breasts on a baking sheet. Spoon the bruschetta mix on top of the chicken breasts.
7. Put the chicken breasts in the oven and cook under the broiler for 3–5 minutes so that the bruschetta mix just starts to brown.
8. To serve, carefully lift the chicken breasts off the baking sheet and onto dinner plates, and sprinkle some fresh basil on top.

Indian Butter Chicken

Butter chicken is a mild Indian curry that is creamy and delicious served over rice.

Ingredients
Serves 6

3 tablespoons butter
1 medium onion, diced
3 cloves garlic, minced
1 tablespoon grated fresh gingerroot
1 tablespoon turmeric
1 tablespoon chili powder
1 tablespoon ground coriander

½ teaspoon ground cinnamon

¼ teaspoon cayenne pepper

1 teaspoon sea salt

1½ cups tomato sauce

2 pounds boneless, skinless chicken breasts, cut into 1" cubes
1 cup heavy cream

⅓ cup minced fresh cilantro

1. Melt the butter in a medium saucepan over medium heat. Add the onion, garlic, and ginger and cook for about 5 minutes, or until the onion is translucent.
2. Stir in the turmeric, chili powder, coriander, cinnamon, cayenne pepper, and salt. Heat for 1–2 minutes so the spices bloom.

3. Pour in the tomato sauce and bring to a low simmer. Cook, stirring often, for about 5–7 minutes. Remove from heat and let cool to room temperature.
4. Fill the water bath with water. Set your sous vide machine temperature to 146°F.
5. Place the chicken in a large bowl, pour in ½ cup of the cooked sauce, and toss to coat the chicken evenly. Place the remaining sauce in the fridge.
6. Pour the coated chicken, along with any sauce from the bowl, in a food-safe bag and vacuum seal the bag. Make sure the chicken cubes are lined up side by side and not stacked or piled. Use multiple bags if necessary.
7. Place the chicken in the water bath and cook sous vide for 2–4 hours.
8. About 10 minutes before the chicken is ready, reheat the remaining sauce in a large saucepan over medium heat.
9. Take the chicken out of the sous vide water bath and place it in the saucepan with the sauce. Pour in the cream, stir, and let the sauce simmer for about 3–4 minutes. Serve over rice and sprinkle the fresh cilantro on top.

Ancho Chicken Fajitas

Chicken breast cooked in the sous vide is tender and ideal for fajitas, and the ancho chilies give them a smoky flavor with a hint of heat.

Ingredients
Serves 4–6

3 dried ancho chilies
1 medium yellow onion, quartered
2 tablespoons olive oil
1 teaspoon sea salt

½ teaspoon black pepper

4 (4-ounce) boneless, skinless chicken breasts
3 tablespoons butter
2 medium red onions, sliced
1 medium red bell pepper, sliced
1 medium yellow bell pepper, sliced
8–12 (8") soft flour tortillas

1½ cups grated Cheddar or Monterey jack cheese

Other toppings like diced tomato, sliced avocado, and sour cream

---

Mixing Up the Aromatics

This recipe uses the smoky taste of ancho chilies in the marinade for the chicken. Marinades are a great way to infuse aromatics into the meat and because sous vide cooking is low and slow, it provides a great opportunity for a deepening of the flavors. There are many options out there, so get creative and try something new!

1. Soak the ancho chilies in hot water for 15 minutes. Remove the stems and discard. Place the ancho chilies in a food processor with the yellow onion, oil, salt, and pepper. Process until a smooth paste forms.
2. Fill the water bath with water. Set your sous vide machine temperature to 146°F.
3. Rub the ancho chili paste all over the chicken breasts.
4. Place the coated chicken in a food-safe bag and vacuum seal the bag. Make sure the chicken is lined up side by side and not stacked or piled. Use multiple bags if necessary.
5. Place the chicken in the water bath and cook sous vide for 1½–4 hours.
6. In a large skillet, melt the butter over medium heat. Add the red onions and bell peppers and cook until tender, about 4–6 minutes.
7. Take the chicken out of the water bath and cut into ¼"-thick slices.
8. Assemble the fajitas by placing some sliced chicken on a soft tortilla. Add some of the sautéed vegetables and the grated cheese. If desired, top with tomato, avocado, or sour cream. Roll up the tortilla and serve. Repeat with the remaining tortillas.

Buffalo Chicken Naan Pizza

Naan bread is the perfect size and shape for personal-sized pizza. The Buffalo sauce gives this pizza a spicy kick and is a nice alternative to a traditional pizza sauce.

Ingredients
Serves 4

1 teaspoon sea salt

½ teaspoon freshly ground black pepper

2 (4-ounce) boneless, skinless chicken breasts

4 pieces naan bread

⅓ cup Buffalo wing hot sauce

½ sweet onion, diced

½ yellow bell pepper, cored and diced

1½ cups grated mozzarella cheese

⅓ cup crumbled blue cheese

1. Sprinkle the salt and pepper on the chicken breasts. Place the chicken breasts in a food-safe bag and vacuum seal it.
2. Fill the water bath with water. Set your sous vide machine temperature to 146°F.
3. Place the chicken in the water bath and cook sous vide for 1½–4 hours.
4. Take the chicken out of the water bath and pat dry with a paper towel. Cut the chicken into small cubes.

5. Preheat the oven to 400°F.
6. Place the naan bread on a baking sheet and brush the Buffalo wing hot sauce on the naan bread. Spread cubed chicken, diced onion, and bell pepper on the naan bread. Sprinkle the grated cheese and crumbled blue cheese on top.
7. Bake the naan pizzas in the oven for 10–15 minutes or until the cheese melts and starts to bubble.
8. Take the pizzas out of the oven and let them rest for 2–3 minutes before serving.

Chicken and Pepperoni Pizza Wraps

Grill these pizza wraps in a panini press and wrap them in aluminum foil for a great on-the-go lunch!

Ingredients
Serves 4–6

1 teaspoon sea salt

½ teaspoon freshly ground black pepper

4 (4-ounce) boneless, skinless chicken breasts
2 tablespoons olive oil
2 medium sweet onions, sliced
1 medium green bell pepper, cored and sliced
2 cups sliced fresh cremini mushrooms
2 cups pizza sauce
1 cup quartered pepperoni slices
8–12 (8") soft flour tortillas

1½ cups grated mozzarella cheese

Mini Pizza Party!

Use the chicken and pepperoni mixture to make mini pizzas with English muffin halves. Place some English muffins cut side up on a baking tray. Spread some of the chicken and pepperoni mixture on the English muffins and top with grated mozzarella and any other desired pizza toppings. Bake in a preheated 375°F oven for 10 minutes.

---

1. Sprinkle the salt and pepper on the chicken breasts. Place the chicken breasts in a food-safe bag and vacuum seal it. Make

sure the chicken is lined up side by side and not stacked or piled. Use multiple bags if necessary.
2. Fill the water bath with water. Set your sous vide machine temperature to 146°F.
3. Place the chicken in the water bath and cook sous vide for 1½–4 hours.
4. In a large skillet, heat the oil over medium heat. Add the onions, bell pepper, and mushrooms and sauté until tender, about 4–6 minutes.
5. Take the chicken out of the water bath and pat dry with a paper towel. Cut into small cubes and place in a large bowl. Pour the pizza sauce and pepperoni on top of the chicken. Mix to combine.
6. Make the wraps by spooning some of the chicken mixture on a soft tortilla. Add some sautéed vegetables and top with mozzarella cheese. Roll up the tortilla. Repeat with the remaining tortillas and serve.

Chicken Shawarmas

This classic Arabic street food, which originated in Turkey, can be made right at home using the sous vide cooking method and the chicken will be tender and delicious.

Ingredients
Serves 6–8

2 tablespoons olive oil
1 tablespoon paprika
2 teaspoons ground cumin

1½ teaspoons ground cardamom

1½ teaspoons salt, divided

½ teaspoon ground allspice

½ teaspoon cayenne pepper

½ teaspoon ground cinnamon
4 (4-ounce) boneless, skinless chicken breasts

½ cup tahini

4 cloves garlic

¾ cup water

⅓ cup lemon juice

6–8 pitas
2 medium tomatoes, thinly sliced
1 large head romaine lettuce, shredded
1 medium sweet onion, thinly sliced

¼ cup minced fresh flat-leaf parsley
2 cups *Pickled Turnips* (see recipe in Chapter 15)
Hot sauce (optional)

1. Make the shawarma spice paste by mixing together the oil, paprika, cumin, cardamom, 1 teaspoon salt, allspice, cayenne, and cinnamon until it resembles a paste.
2. Rub the shawarma spice paste all over the chicken breasts. Place the chicken breasts in a food-safe bag and vacuum seal it. Make sure the chicken is lined up side by side and not stacked or piled. Use multiple bags if necessary. If desired, let the chicken marinate in the fridge for 1–2 hours before cooking them in the sous vide.
3. Fill the water bath with water. Set your sous vide machine temperature to 146°F.
4. Place the chicken in the water bath and cook sous vide for 1½–4 hours.
5. Make the tahini garlic sauce by placing the tahini, garlic cloves, water, lemon juice, and remaining ½ teaspoon salt in a food processor or blender. Process on high until smooth and creamy. Add a little bit of extra water if a thinner sauce is desired.
6. Take the chicken out of the water bath and cut into ¼" slices.
7. To make a shawarma, open up half of the pita round from the edge and fold back. Spread some tahini paste inside the pita bread. Add some of the sliced chicken, tomatoes, romaine lettuce, onion, a little bit of minced parsley, pickled turnips, and, if desired, a few drops of hot sauce. Wrap up the pita and serve. Repeat with the remaining pita bread.

Chicken Cacciatore

This hearty tomato-based chicken recipe is a classic hunter-style Italian dish and is great served on a bed of fresh pasta.

Ingredients
Serves 4–6

2 teaspoons sea salt, divided

½ teaspoon freshly ground black pepper

4 (4-ounce) boneless, skinless chicken breasts
2 tablespoons olive oil
1 medium yellow onion, diced
1 medium red bell pepper, cored and diced
3 cloves garlic, minced
4 cups marinara sauce
1 cup pitted green olives
1 tablespoon granulated sugar
1 teaspoon dried basil
1 teaspoon dried oregano

1½–2 pounds dry pasta (penne, rotini, spaghetti, etc.)
Grated Parmesan cheese (optional)

1. Sprinkle 1 teaspoon of the salt and pepper on the chicken breasts. Place the chicken breasts in a food-safe bag and vacuum seal it. Make sure the chicken is lined up side by side and not stacked or piled. Use multiple bags if necessary.
2. Fill the water bath with water. Set your sous vide machine temperature to 146°F.

3. Place the chicken in the water bath and cook sous vide for 1½–4 hours.
4. In a large skillet, heat the oil over medium heat. Add the onion, pepper, and garlic and sauté until tender, about 4–6 minutes. Add the marinara sauce, green olives, sugar, basil, oregano, and salt. Bring to a boil and then lower the heat. Let the sauce simmer for about 45 minutes.
5. Cook the pasta according to the directions on the package. Drain.
6. Take the chicken out of the water bath and cut into ¼"-thick slices.
7. To serve, spoon some of the cacciatore sauce over a bed of cooked pasta. Place some sliced chicken on top of the sauce, and spoon a little more sauce over the chicken. If desired, sprinkle some Parmesan cheese on top.

Barbecue Chicken on a Bun

There is no need for a grill to make an awesome chicken sandwich and this sous vide version is tender and coated with plenty of barbecue sauce.

Ingredients
Serves 4

4 (4-ounce) boneless, skinless chicken breasts

1½ cups barbecue sauce, divided
4 crusty kaiser rolls, cut in half
4 slices cheese (Cheddar, Swiss, mozzarella, etc.)
1 large tomato, sliced
1 large red onion, sliced
4–8 large lettuce leaves

1. Carefully slice the chicken breast in half horizontally so that it is 2 flat pieces of chicken. Do this with the remaining chicken breasts. In a medium bowl, toss the sliced chicken breasts in 1 cup of the barbecue sauce.
2. Place the barbecue-coated chicken breast slices in a food-safe bag and vacuum seal it. If necessary, use a spatula to scrape all the sauce out of the bowl and into the bag. Make sure the chicken slices are lined up side by side and not stacked or piled. Use multiple bags if necessary.
3. Fill the water bath with water. Set your sous vide machine temperature to 146°F.
4. Place the chicken in the water bath and cook sous vide for 1–2 hours.
5. Take the chicken out of the water bath.

6. Assemble the sandwiches by placing 2 slices of the cooked chicken breast on each bun. Spread a little bit of the remaining ½ cup barbecue sauce on the chicken of each of the 4 sandwiches. Top each with a slice of cheese, tomato, onion, and 1–2 leaves of lettuce.

Crispy Hoisin-Glazed Chicken Drumsticks

This Asian glaze is sweet and sticky with a hint of spice. The toasted sesame seeds stick to the sauce and add a nice flavor to the chicken.

Ingredients
Serves 4–6

6 tablespoons hoisin sauce, divided
5 tablespoons soy sauce, divided

¼ cup rice vinegar, divided

2 tablespoons sesame oil, divided
12 chicken drumsticks
2 tablespoons honey
1 teaspoon sriracha sauce
Vegetable oil, as needed
2 tablespoons toasted sesame seeds

Twice Cooked

The combination of sous vide and a deep fryer can ensure that the chicken drumstick is juicy and perfectly cooked while the skin it crispy and delicious! This method is also used to create some of the best chicken wings around.

1. In a large bowl, whisk together 3 tablespoons hoisin sauce, 3 tablespoons soy sauce, 2 tablespoons vinegar, and 1 tablespoon sesame oil. Toss the drumsticks in the marinade mixture.
2. Place the coated chicken drumsticks and the marinade in a food-safe bag and vacuum seal it. Make sure the chicken is

lined up side by side and not stacked or piled. Use multiple bags if necessary. If desired, let the chicken marinate in the fridge for 1–2 hours before cooking them in the sous vide.
3. Fill the water bath with water. Set your sous vide machine temperature to 176°F.
4. Place the chicken in the water bath and cook sous vide for 4–6 hours.
5. In a medium saucepan, heat the remaining hoisin sauce, soy sauce, rice vinegar, and sesame oil with the honey and sriracha sauce on medium. Let it simmer for about 5–10 minutes so that it thickens to a nice glaze consistency. Set the hoisin glaze aside.
6. Take the chicken drumsticks out of the bag and pat dry with a paper towel.
7. Heat the oil in a deep fryer to 400°F. Place the drumsticks in the deep fryer just long enough to crisp up the skin, 2–3 minutes. Drain on a paper towel.
8. Toss the crispy drumsticks in the hoisin glaze and sprinkle with toasted sesame seeds.

Crispy Hoisin-Glazed Chicken Drumsticks

Crispy Barbecue Chicken Drumsticks

Crispy on the outside, juicy in the middle, and tossed in barbecue sauce, these chicken drumsticks are as good as they get!

Ingredients
Serves 4–6

2 teaspoons paprika
2 teaspoons garlic powder
2 teaspoons sea salt
12 chicken drumsticks
2 tablespoons hot sauce
Vegetable oil, as needed
1 cup barbecue sauce

1. Sprinkle the paprika, garlic powder, and salt all over the chicken drumsticks.
2. Place the spiced chicken drumsticks and hot sauce in a food-safe bag and vacuum seal it. Make sure the chicken is lined up side by side and not stacked or piled. Use multiple bags if necessary. If desired, let the chicken marinate in the fridge for 1–2 hours before cooking them in the sous vide.
3. Fill the water bath with water. Set your sous vide machine temperature to 176°F.
4. Place the chicken in the water bath and cook sous vide for 4–6 hours.
5. Take the chicken drumsticks out of the bag and pat dry with a paper towel.
6. Heat the oil in a deep fryer to 400°F. Place the drumsticks in the deep fryer just long enough to crisp up the skin, 2–3

minutes. Drain on a paper towel.
7. Toss the crispy drumsticks in the barbecue sauce and serve.

Crispy Sous Vide Chicken Wings

Making sous vide chicken wings results in moist and tender meat and super crispy skin.

Ingredients
Serves 4

2 pounds whole chicken wings

½ cup all-purpose flour

1 teaspoon sea salt

½ teaspoon black pepper

1. Cut the chicken wings into 3 pieces. Keep the drumettes and wingettes (flats), but throw away the wing tips.
2. Fill the water bath with water. Set your sous vide machine temperature to 176°F.
3. Place the chicken wing pieces in a food-safe bag and vacuum seal the bag. Make sure they are lined up side by side and not stacked or piled. Use multiple bags if necessary.
4. Place the chicken wings in the water bath and cook sous vide for 3 hours.
5. Remove the chicken wings from the bag and pat dry with a paper towel.
6. Dredge the wings in the flour. Shake off excess flour and deep-fry the chicken in 350°F oil for about 8–10 minutes.
7. Place the wings on paper towels to remove the excess oil. Sprinkle salt and pepper on the wings.

Chapter 9
Beef

The Perfect Steak

These simple instructions will allow you to cook a steak that is as good as one you would pay plenty of money for at a high-end steak house.

Ingredients
Serves 1

- 1 steak, 1" thick (strip loin, sirloin, rib eye, or other boneless steak)
- 1 tablespoon oil with a high smoke point (like peanut, sunflower, corn, vegetable, or safflower oil)
- 1 tablespoon butter
- ½ teaspoon sea salt
- ¼ teaspoon freshly ground black pepper

> **Up to Your Personal Preference**
>
> Everyone has their own preference for how they like their steaks prepared. Therefore, the temperature guide in *Appendix A* shows a range for each level of doneness. After a number of tests, I discovered that my personal favorite steak is cooked at 133°F. Use the guide as a resource and try different temperatures to see what you like best.

1. Fill the water bath with water. Set your sous vide machine temperature to 134°F for medium rare. If a different doneness for steak is desired, check *Appendix A: Time and Temperature Charts*.
2. Place the steak in a food-safe bag and vacuum seal the bag.
3. Place the steak in the water bath and cook sous vide for a minimum of 1 hour. For thicker steaks, refer to *Appendix A:*

Time and Temperature Charts. Do not worry about cooking the steak too long, as it is impossible to overcook the steak; once the core of the steak reaches the temperature of the water, it will hold there.

4. Remove the steak from the bag and pat dry with a paper towel.
5. Heat the oil in a medium skillet on high heat. Sear the steak in the skillet for about 45–60 seconds per side. While the steak is searing, add the butter to the skillet and use a spoon to baste the melted butter on top of the steak.
6. Remove the steak from the skillet and sprinkle with the salt and pepper.
7. Let rest for 3–4 minutes. Serve.

The Perfect Steak

Steak with Herb Compound Butter

This simple recipe strips away any extra flavors and showcases the meat. Change things up by substituting the herbs in the butter or switching the lemon juice with lime, or adding some minced garlic.

Ingredients
Serves 4

4 steaks (strip loin, sirloin, rib eye, or other boneless steak), 1" thick

½ cup salted butter, softened

3 tablespoons minced fresh chives

1 tablespoon minced fresh rosemary

2 teaspoons lemon juice

2 tablespoons oil with a high smoke point (like peanut, sunflower, corn, vegetable, or safflower oil)

1 teaspoon sea salt

½ teaspoon freshly ground black pepper

More or Less Servings

While this and many of the other steak recipes in this chapter are written to serve 4, it is easy to modify it to serve more or less. In the case of this compound butter, any extra can stay in the fridge for about 1 week or in the freezer for up to 6 months. Compound butter is also great on sous vide salmon or chicken breast.

---

1. Fill the water bath with water. Set your sous vide machine temperature to 134°F for medium rare. If a different doneness

for steak is desired, check *Appendix A: Time and Temperature Charts*.
2. Place the steaks in a food-safe bag and vacuum seal the bag. Make sure the steaks are lined up side by side and not stacked or piled. Use multiple bags if necessary.
3. Place the steaks in the water bath and cook sous vide for a minimum of 1 hour.
4. Make the compound butter by mixing together the softened butter, fresh chives, rosemary, and lemon juice in a small bowl. Form into a long cylinder that is about 1½" in diameter. Roll the butter in plastic wrap and twist the ends. Place in the fridge for the butter to harden.
5. Remove the steaks from the bag and pat dry with a paper towel.
6. Heat the oil in a large skillet over high heat. Sear the steak in the skillet for about 45–60 seconds per side.
7. Remove the steak from the skillet and sprinkle with the salt and pepper.
8. Take the compound butter out of the fridge and remove the plastic wrap. Slice the butter into ¼–1/2" rounds.
9. Put each steak on a dinner plate and top with 2–3 slices of the compound butter. Serve.

Steak with Herb Compound Butter

Steak and Scallops with Chipotle Cream

This recipe is one of the more complex ones in this chapter but it is well worth it. The flavors blend together to create a dish that will be extremely memorable!

Ingredients
Serves 4

12 large sea scallops
4 steaks (strip loin, sirloin, rib eye, or other boneless steak), 1" thick
3 tablespoons butter
2 medium shallots, minced
2 medium chipotle peppers in adobo sauce

1½ cups heavy cream

½ cup grated Parmesan cheese

2 teaspoons sea salt, divided
2 tablespoons oil with a high smoke point (like peanut, sunflower, corn, vegetable, or safflower oil)

½ teaspoon freshly ground black pepper

2 tablespoons minced fresh flat-leaf parsley

1. Fill the water bath with water. Set your sous vide machine temperature to 140°F.
2. Place the scallops in a food-safe bag and vacuum seal the bag. Make sure the scallops are lined up side by side and not stacked or piled. Use multiple bags if necessary.

3. Place the scallops in the water bath and cook sous vide for 40–60 minutes.
4. After the sous vide cooking session, place the bag in an ice bath to chill immediately. Place in the fridge.
5. Adjust the sous vide machine temperature to 134°F for medium rare. If a different doneness for steak is desired, check *Appendix A: Time and Temperature Charts*.
6. Place the steaks in a food-safe bag and vacuum seal the bag. Make sure the steaks are lined up side by side and not stacked or piled. Use multiple bags if necessary.
7. Place the steaks in the water bath and cook sous vide for a minimum of 1 hour.
8. To make the chipotle cream sauce, melt the butter in a medium saucepan over medium heat. Add the minced shallots and cook until tender, about 3–4 minutes. Add the chipotle peppers, heavy cream, and Parmesan cheese. Cook for 5–6 minutes, ensuring that the sauce does not boil. Use an immersion blender to purée the sauce. Stir in 1 teaspoon of salt and let the sauce simmer for a few minutes to thicken. Remove from heat and cover.
9. With 4–5 minutes cooking time left for the steak, place the scallops bag in the water bath with the steak to warm them.
10. Remove the steaks from the bag and pat dry with a paper towel.
11. Heat 1 tablespoon oil in a large skillet over high heat. Sear the steak in the skillet for about 45–60 seconds per side. Remove steak from the skillet and sprinkle with some of the salt and pepper. Clean the skillet.
12. Remove the scallops from the bag and pat dry with a paper towel.
13. Heat the remaining 1 tablespoon oil in a large skillet over high heat. Sear the scallops in the skillet for about 30 seconds per side. Remove the scallops from the skillet and sprinkle with the remaining salt and pepper.

14. To serve, place each steak on a dinner plate. Put 3 scallops on top of each steak and pour some of the chipotle cream over the scallops and steak. Sprinkle some minced parsley on top and serve.

Steak with Serrano Chili Chimichurri

This spicy version of the classic Argentinian steak sauce is simple to make, packed with fresh flavors, and perfectly complements the tenderness of sous vide steak.

Ingredients
Serves 4

- 4 steaks (strip loin, sirloin, rib eye, or other boneless steak), 1" thick
- 1 packed cup fresh flat-leaf parsley leaves
- 3–4 medium serrano peppers, cored and seeded
- 2 cloves garlic
- 1 tablespoon minced fresh oregano
- ¼ cup lemon juice
- ¼ cup olive oil
- 2 teaspoons sea salt, divided
- 2 tablespoons oil with a high smoke point (like peanut, sunflower, corn, vegetable, or safflower oil)
- ½ teaspoon freshly ground black pepper

A Chimichurri Twist

Switch up some of the ingredients to give this sauce a unique twist. Replace the fresh parsley with cilantro, the fresh oregano with mint, and substitute the lemon juice with lime juice. These modifications work really well to both change up the sauce and brighten up the flavor of the steak.

1. Fill the water bath with water. Set your sous vide machine temperature to 134°F for medium rare. If a different doneness for steak is desired, check *Appendix A: Time and Temperature Charts*.
2. Place the steaks in a food-safe bag and vacuum seal the bag. Make sure the steaks are lined up side by side and not stacked or piled. Use multiple bags if necessary.
3. Place the steaks in the water bath and cook sous vide for a minimum of 1 hour.
4. Make the chimichurri by placing the parsley, serrano peppers, garlic, oregano, lemon juice, olive oil, and 1 teaspoon of the salt in a food processor bowl. Pulse until everything is evenly and finely minced. It should be fairly smooth and resemble pesto in consistency. Pour into a small bowl, cover with plastic wrap, and place in the fridge for 1 hour to allow the flavors to develop.
5. Remove the steaks from the bag and pat dry with a paper towel.
6. Heat the oil in a large skillet over high heat. Sear the steaks in the skillet for about 45–60 seconds per side.
7. Remove the steaks from the skillet and sprinkle with the remaining salt and the pepper.
8. Put each steak on a dinner plate and spoon some chimichurri sauce on top. Serve.

Steak with Tropical Salsa

The bright, fresh flavor of the tropical salsa perfectly complements the deep rich taste of the steak.

Ingredients
Serves 4

- 4 steaks (strip loin, sirloin, rib eye, or other boneless steak), 1" thick
- 1 cup quartered grape tomatoes
- 1 cup finely diced pineapple
- 1 medium jalapeño, cored and minced
- ¼ medium red onion, minced
- 1 tablespoon minced fresh mint
- 2 tablespoons lime juice
- 2 tablespoons oil with a high smoke point (like peanut, sunflower, corn, vegetable, or safflower oil)
- 1 teaspoon sea salt
- ½ teaspoon freshly ground black pepper

1. Fill the water bath with water. Set your sous vide machine temperature to 134°F for medium rare. If a different doneness for steak is desired, check *Appendix A: Time and Temperature Charts*.
2. Place the steaks in a food-safe bag and vacuum seal the bag. Make sure the steaks are lined up side by side and not stacked or piled. Use multiple bags if necessary.
3. Place the steaks in the water bath and cook sous vide for a minimum of 1 hour.

4. Make the salsa by mixing together the grape tomatoes, pineapple, jalapeño, red onion, mint, and lime juice in a medium bowl. Cover with plastic wrap and place in the fridge for 1 hour to allow the flavors to develop.
5. Remove the steaks from the bag and pat dry with a paper towel.
6. Heat the oil in a large skillet on high heat. Sear the steaks in the skillet for about 45–60 seconds per side.
7. Remove the steaks from the skillet and sprinkle with salt and pepper.
8. Put each steak on a dinner plate and spoon some tropical salsa on top. Serve.

Steak with Bourbon Mushroom Sauce

A little bit of bourbon adds a wonderful aromatic to the sauce, which then highlights the taste of the steak.

Ingredients
Serves 4

- 4 steaks (strip loin, sirloin, rib eye, or other boneless steak), 1" thick
- 3 tablespoons butter
- 3 cups sliced cremini or button mushrooms
- 1 medium sweet onion, thinly sliced

- ½ cup beef broth
- 1 tablespoon soy sauce
- 2–3 tablespoons bourbon
- 2 tablespoons oil with a high smoke point (like peanut, sunflower, corn, vegetable, or safflower oil)
- 1 teaspoon sea salt
- ½ teaspoon freshly ground black pepper

1. Fill the water bath with water. Set your sous vide machine temperature to 134°F for medium rare. If a different doneness for steak is desired, check *Appendix A: Time and Temperature Charts*.
2. Place the steaks in a food-safe bag and vacuum seal the bag. Make sure the steaks are lined up side by side and not stacked or piled. Use multiple bags if necessary.
3. Place the steaks in the water bath and cook sous vide for a minimum of 1 hour.

4. Make the mushroom sauce by melting the butter in a medium skillet over medium heat. Add the mushrooms and onion and sauté until the onion is transparent and the mushrooms are tender, about 4–6 minutes. Pour in the beef broth, soy sauce, and bourbon. Bring to a boil and then lower the heat to a simmer. Let the sauce simmer for about 10 minutes so that it reduces and thickens. Remove from heat.
5. Remove the steaks from the bag and pat dry with a paper towel.
6. Heat the oil in a large skillet over high heat. Sear the steaks in the skillet for about 45–60 seconds per side.
7. Remove the steaks from the skillet and sprinkle with salt and pepper.
8. Put each steak on a dinner plate and spoon some mushroom sauce on top. Serve.

Flank Steak Banh Mi Sandwiches with Sriracha Lime Mayo

This classic Vietnamese version of a sub or hoagie has layers upon layers of flavors. Tender meat, sour pickled vegetables, and spicy mayo make this one special sandwich.

Ingredients
Serves 4

- 1 (2-pound) flank steak
- 1½ teaspoons sea salt
- 1 teaspoon freshly ground black pepper
- 1 cup mayonnaise
- 2–3 tablespoons sriracha sauce
- 3–4 tablespoons lime juice
- 1 tablespoon honey
- 2 tablespoons oil with a high smoke point (like peanut, sunflower, corn, vegetable, or safflower oil)
- 4 small (10") French baguettes, cut in half lengthwise
- 2 medium tomatoes, sliced
- Small handful romaine lettuce leaves
- Small handful cilantro leaves
- 1 cup *Vietnamese Pickled Carrots and Daikon* (see recipe in Chapter 15)

1. Fill the water bath with water. Set your sous vide machine temperature to 135°F.
2. Rub the flank steak all over with the salt and pepper. Place the steak in a food-safe bag and vacuum seal the bag.

3. Place the steak in the water bath and cook sous vide for 12–18 hours.
4. Make the sriracha lime mayo by whisking together the mayonnaise, sriracha sauce, lime juice, and honey in a medium bowl until smooth. Cover with plastic wrap and place in the fridge.
5. Remove the steak from the bag and pat dry with a paper towel.
6. Heat the oil in a large skillet over high heat. Sear the steaks in the skillet for about 45–60 seconds per side.
7. Let the steak rest for 5 minutes. Cut the flank steak against the grain into thin slices.
8. Assemble the banh mi sandwiches by spreading some sriracha lime mayo on the inside of the baguettes. Place some flank steak slices in the baguettes along with some tomato slices, romaine leaves, and a few cilantro leaves. Top with some Vietnamese Pickled Carrots and Daikon. If desired, squirt a little extra sriracha sauce on top.

Coffee and Chocolate Flank Steak Tacos

The bold flavors of coffee and chocolate on the flank steak complement the bright taste of the guacamole.

Ingredients
Serves 4–6

1 tablespoon ground espresso or dark coffee, finely ground

1½ teaspoons cocoa powder

1 tablespoon light brown sugar

½ teaspoon sea salt

½ teaspoon dry mustard

¼ teaspoon ground cinnamon

¼ teaspoon cayenne pepper

1 (2-pound) flank steak
3 ripe medium avocados
2 medium tomatoes, diced
3 green onions, thinly sliced

¼ cup chopped fresh cilantro

2 medium limes
3 tablespoons vegetable oil
12 (6") soft flour tortillas

> **How Much Rub?**
>
> Sous vide cooking requires less rub on the meat than other cooking methods, like grilling or searing, because the meat is sealed in with those spices over a much longer time.

1. Make the rub by mixing together the ground espresso, cocoa powder, brown sugar, salt, dry mustard, cinnamon, and cayenne pepper in a small bowl.
2. Fill the water bath with water. Set your sous vide machine temperature to 135°F.
3. Rub the flank steak all over with the spice rub. Place the steak in a food-safe bag and vacuum seal the bag.
4. Place the steak in the water bath and cook sous vide for 12–18 hours.
5. Make the guacamole while the steak is in the water bath. Cut the avocados in half, remove the pit, and scoop the avocado flesh into a medium bowl. Mash the avocado with a potato masher or fork until fairly creamy. Add the tomatoes, green onions, and cilantro to the bowl. Squeeze the juice of 1 lime into the bowl. Stir until well incorporated.
6. Remove the steak from the bag and pat dry with a paper towel.
7. Heat the oil in a large skillet over high heat. Sear the steak in the skillet for about 45–60 seconds per side.
8. Cut the flank steak against the grain into thin slices.
9. Assemble the tacos by placing a few slices of the steak on each tortilla. Spoon a dollop of guacamole and squeeze a little bit of lime juice on top.

Double-Seared Beef Tenderloin

By searing the beef tenderloin both before and after it is cooked in the sous vide water bath, the flavor is deepened and intensified.

Ingredients
Serves 4

1 trimmed center-cut beef tenderloin (about 1½–2 pounds), 2" in diameter, cut in half lengthwise

2 tablespoons oil with a high smoke point, divided (like peanut, sunflower, corn, vegetable, or safflower oil)

2 tablespoons butter

½ teaspoon sea salt

¼ teaspoon freshly ground black pepper

1. If desired, use kitchen string to tie around each of the beef tenderloin pieces. Do this at 3 places and it will ensure an evenly round finished product.
2. Heat 1 tablespoon of the oil in a large skillet over medium-high heat.
3. Add the beef tenderloin pieces to the skillet and sear for about 30–60 seconds per side. Rotate the tenderloin and sear all sides.
4. Place the beef tenderloin pieces in separate food-safe bags and, before sealing, place them into an ice bath to chill the meat. Make sure that the opening of the bag does not go under the ice water or water will enter into the bag. Once chilled, vacuum seal the bag.

5. Fill the water bath with water. Set your sous vide machine temperature to 134°F for medium rare. If a different doneness for beef is desired, check *Appendix A: Time and Temperature Charts*.
6. Place the beef tenderloin in the water bath and cook sous vide for 3–4 hours.
7. Remove the beef tenderloin from the bag and pat dry with a paper towel.
8. Heat the remaining tablespoon of oil in a large skillet over high heat. Sear the tenderloin in the skillet for about 45–60 seconds per side.
9. While the tenderloin is searing, add the butter to the skillet and use a spoon to baste the melted butter on top of the beef tenderloin.
10. Remove the beef tenderloin from the skillet and sprinkle with salt and pepper.
11. Let rest for 3–4 minutes. Slice and serve.

Beef Tenderloin Medallions on Creamed Spinach and Potato Mash

This full dinner is something that could be ordered at a fine-dining restaurant. The beef is tender, the spinach is creamy, and everything is super simple to make.

Ingredients
Serves 4

1 trimmed center-cut beef tenderloin (about 1½–2 pounds)

¼ cup butter, divided

2 medium shallots, minced
1 clove garlic, minced
4–6 cups fresh baby spinach
1 cup heavy cream

⅓ cup grated Parmesan cheese

1 teaspoon sea salt, divided

½ teaspoon freshly ground black pepper, divided

⅛ teaspoon cayenne pepper

1 tablespoon oil with a high smoke point (like peanut, sunflower, corn, vegetable, or safflower oil)

4 cups *Mashed Potatoes* (for sous vide recipe, see Chapter 13)

1. Cut the beef tenderloin into 4 equal medallions (the medallions should be 1" thick).
2. Place the beef in a food-safe bag and vacuum seal the bags. Make sure the beef is lined up side by side and not stacked or

piled. Use multiple bags if necessary.
3. Fill the water bath with water. Set your sous vide machine temperature to 134°F for medium rare. If a different doneness for beef is desired, check _Appendix A: Time and Temperature Charts_.
4. Place the beef in the water bath and cook sous vide for a minimum of 1 hour.
5. About 30 minutes before the beef is done, make the creamed spinach by heating 2 tablespoons of the butter in a medium saucepan over medium heat. Add the shallots along with the garlic and cook until tender, about 4 minutes. Add the spinach and cook until wilted and tender. Stir in the heavy cream, Parmesan cheese, ½ teaspoon salt, ¼ teaspoon black pepper, and cayenne pepper. Simmer and stir until the cream thickens, about 4–5 minutes. Remove from heat.
6. Remove the beef tenderloin from the bag and pat dry with a paper towel.
7. Heat the oil in a medium skillet over high heat. Sear the beef medallions in the skillet for about 45–60 seconds per side. While the beef is searing, add the remaining 2 tablespoons of butter to the skillet and use a spoon to baste the beef tenderloin with the melted butter.
8. Remove the beef medallions from the skillet and sprinkle with the remaining salt and pepper. Let rest for 3–4 minutes.
9. To serve, spoon some mashed potatoes on a plate, top with some creamed spinach, and place a beef medallion on top or next to the spinach.

Beef Tenderloin Medallions with Red Wine and Portobello Mushroom Sauce

This recipe is decadent, as the beef is so tender, it will melt in your mouth. The mushroom sauce has the deep flavor of the reduced wine.

Ingredients
Serves 4

1 trimmed center-cut beef tenderloin (about 1½–2 pounds)

¼ cup butter, divided

2 medium shallots, minced
1 clove garlic, minced
5 cups sliced portobello mushrooms
1 cup dry red wine
1 cup beef broth
1 teaspoon sea salt, divided

½ teaspoon freshly ground black pepper, divided

1 tablespoon oil with a high smoke point, divided (like peanut, sunflower, corn, vegetable, or safflower oil)

1. Cut the beef tenderloin into 4 equal medallions (the medallions should be 1" thick).
2. Place the beef in a food-safe bag and vacuum seal the bag. Make sure the beef is lined up side by side and not stacked or piled. Use multiple bags if necessary.
3. Fill the water bath with water. Set your sous vide machine temperature to 134°F for medium rare. If a different doneness

for steak is desired, check *Appendix A: Time and Temperature Charts*.
4. Place the beef in the water bath and cook sous vide for a minimum of 1 hour.
5. About 30 minutes before the beef is done cooking, make the red wine and portobello mushroom sauce by heating 2 tablespoons of the butter in a medium saucepan over medium heat. Add the shallots along with the garlic and cook until tender, about 4 minutes. Add the sliced mushrooms and cook until tender. Pour in the red wine and beef broth. Stirring often, let it simmer and reduce for about 10 minutes. Sprinkle in ½ teaspoon of the salt and ¼ teaspoon black pepper. Remove from the heat.
6. Remove the beef tenderloin from the bag and pat dry with a paper towel.
7. Heat the oil in a large skillet over high heat. Sear the tenderloins in the skillet for about 45–60 seconds per side. While the beef is searing, add the remaining 2 tablespoons of butter to the skillet, and use a spoon to baste the beef medallions with the melted butter.
8. Remove the beef medallions from the skillet and sprinkle with the remaining salt and pepper. Let rest for 3–4 minutes.
9. To serve, place each beef medallion on a plate and top with some of the red wine and portobello mushroom sauce.

Beer-Braised Beef and Swiss Melt

The low and slow cooking of the sous vide water bath results in super-tender beef that is ideal on this hot beef sandwich.

Ingredients
Serves 6–8

3 tablespoons vegetable oil
2 pounds stewing beef, cut into 1" cubes
1 cup stout beer
1 tablespoon tomato paste
1 teaspoon sea salt
1 teaspoon freshly ground black pepper
2 tablespoons butter
2 medium sweet onions, thinly sliced
1 medium green bell pepper, cored and sliced
1 medium red bell pepper, cored and sliced
6–8 fresh crusty rolls (panini or kaiser)
2 cups grated Swiss cheese

Make-Ahead Meal

This recipe is a great option to make ahead. Simply follow the first 5 steps and then take the bag of meat out of the sous vide water bath and chill it in an ice bath. Then the meat can be placed in the fridge or even freezer for later. To serve, simply reheat the meat and follow the remaining steps to make the beef melts.

1. Heat the oil in a large skillet over medium-high heat. Add the stewing beef to the skillet and sear for about 30–60 seconds

per side. Sear the beef in batches so that the skillet is not overloaded. Chill the seared beef.
2. In a medium saucepan, heat the beer, tomato paste, salt, and pepper and bring to a boil. Let the sauce simmer at a low rolling boil for about 5–7 minutes. Cool to room temperature.
3. Fill the water bath with water. Set your sous vide machine temperature to 145°F.
4. Place the beef and the beer mixture in a food-safe bag and vacuum seal the bag. Make sure the beef is lined up side by side and not stacked or piled. Use multiple bags if necessary.
5. Place the beef in the water bath and cook sous vide for 18–24 hours.
6. Just before the beef is ready to come out of the water bath, melt the butter in a medium skillet over medium heat. Add the sliced onions and peppers and cook until tender, about 7–9 minutes. Remove from heat.
7. Take the beef out of the water bath, open the bag, and pour it into a large bowl.
8. Preheat the oven to broil.
9. Cut the crusty buns in half lengthwise. Do not slice them all the way through. Place them on their side on a large baking sheet and open them up. Place some beef cubes in the opening of the crusty buns and then top with some sautéed onions and peppers. If desired, spoon some of the beer broth that was in the bag with the beef over the beef and veggies. Sprinkle some grated cheese on top.
10. Place in the oven and broil for a few minutes, or until the cheese melts and is starting to bubble. Serve.

Beef Goulash

This classic Hungarian dish has tender stewed meat with a rich tomato sauce served on a bed of egg noodles.

Ingredients
Serves 4–6

4½ tablespoons Hungarian paprika, divided

2½ teaspoons sea salt, divided

1 teaspoon freshly ground black pepper, divided

2–3 pounds stewing beef, cut into 1" cubes

3 tablespoons vegetable oil

¼ cup tomato paste

2 tablespoons butter

2 medium yellow onions, diced

2 cloves garlic, minced

1 cup dry red wine

2 cups crushed tomatoes

2 cups beef broth

1 teaspoon caraway seeds

1 (16-ounce) package egg noodles, cooked

¾ cup sour cream

2 tablespoons minced fresh flat-leaf parsley

1. Make the spice rub by mixing together 2 tablespoons Hungarian paprika, 1½ teaspoons salt, and ½ teaspoon pepper in a shallow bowl. Toss the stewing beef in the spice rub.

2. Heat the oil in a large skillet over medium-high heat. Add the stewing beef to the skillet and sear for about 30–60 seconds per side. Sear the beef in batches so that the skillet is not overloaded. Chill the seared beef.
3. Fill the water bath with water. Set your sous vide machine temperature to 145°F.
4. Place the beef cubes and tomato paste in a food-safe bag and vacuum seal the bag. Make sure the beef is lined up side by side and not stacked or piled. Use multiple bags if necessary.
5. Place the beef in the water bath and cook sous vide for 18–24 hours.
6. About 1 hour before the beef is finished cooking, prepare the goulash sauce. Melt the butter in a large saucepan over medium heat. Add the onions and garlic and cook until tender, for 3 –4 minutes. Add the red wine and let it boil for about 5 minutes. Stir in the crushed tomatoes, beef broth, caraway seeds, and the remaining paprika, salt, and pepper. Let the sauce simmer for about 30 minutes.
7. Pour the contents of the bag (beef and any liquid) to the saucepan. Stir the meat into the sauce and let it simmer on low heat for 5–10 minutes.
8. To serve, spoon the goulash on a bed of cooked egg noodles. Top with a dollop of sour cream and sprinkle some minced parsley on top.

Short Ribs with Pearl Onions and Balsamic Reduction

Tender short ribs with a rich balsamic reduction and sweet pearl onions—this dish is sure to awe your guests. Turn this into a meal by serving it over mashed potatoes or even polenta.

Ingredients
Serves 4

3 pounds short ribs, cut into 1½" individual portions

2½ teaspoons sea salt, divided

1½ teaspoons freshly ground black pepper, divided

3 tablespoons vegetable oil

1½ pounds pearl onions

3 tablespoons butter

½ cup balsamic vinegar

½ cup beef broth

Going the Traditional Way

By changing the temperature of the water bath and the cook time, short ribs can have a very different texture and color. Cooking them at 185°F for 12–18 hours will result in short ribs that have the taste and texture of a traditional braised rib.

---

1. Season the short ribs with 1½ teaspoons sea salt and 1 teaspoon black pepper.

2. Heat the oil in a large skillet over medium-high heat. Add the short ribs to the skillet and sear for about 30–60 seconds per side. Sear the ribs in batches so that the skillet is not overloaded. Chill the seared short ribs.
3. Place the short ribs in a food-safe bag and vacuum seal the bag. Make sure the beef is lined up side by side and not stacked or piled. Use multiple bags if necessary.
4. Fill the water bath with water. Set your sous vide machine temperature to 160°F.
5. Place the short ribs in the water bath and cook sous vide for 24 hours.
6. About 30 minutes before the short ribs are done cooking, place the pearl onions in a small pot of boiling water and blanch for 2–3 minutes. Drain and rinse under cold water to cool. Cut off the ends of the pearl onions and squeeze so the outer peel comes off.
7. Heat the butter in a medium skillet over medium heat and add the onions. Sauté the pearl onions for 2–3 minutes. Pour in the balsamic vinegar and beef broth. Bring to a boil and then lower to a simmer. Let the sauce thicken, stirring often, until it reduces by at least half, about 15 minutes. Remove from heat.
8. Remove the short ribs from the bag and pat dry with a paper towel.
9. Preheat oven to broil.
10. Place the short ribs on a broiling pan or baking sheet with a rack. Make sure the ribs are bone side down. Place the ribs under the broiler for about 3 minutes. Sprinkle with the remaining salt and pepper. Let rest for 1–2 minutes.
11. To serve, place a short rib on each plate and top with some of the pearl onions and balsamic reduction sauce.

Deconstructed Cuban Boliche

This modern take on a classic Cuban dish has super-tender eye of round roast topped with a chorizo and tomato sauce and fried plantains.

Ingredients
Serves 6–8

1½ teaspoons ground cumin

1½ teaspoons dried oregano

1½ teaspoons paprika

1½ teaspoons garlic powder

½ teaspoon cayenne pepper
1 teaspoon freshly ground black pepper
2 teaspoons sea salt, divided
1 eye of round beef roast (about 4 pounds)
3 cloves garlic
1 medium sweet onion, roughly chopped
1 medium red bell pepper, cored and roughly chopped
1 jalapeño pepper, cored and roughly chopped
Small handful of cilantro stems
1 (28-ounce) can diced tomatoes
5 tablespoons vegetable oil, divided
2 pounds fresh chorizo, removed from casings

¾ cup dry white wine

2 tablespoons lime juice

2 tablespoons orange juice

3 tablespoons minced fresh cilantro

2 plantains, peeled and cut into ¼" slices

1. Make the spice rub by mixing together the cumin, oregano, paprika, garlic powder, cayenne, black pepper, and 1 teaspoon salt.
2. Trim any fat or membrane on the outside of the roast. Slice the roast into 1½"-thick medallions.
3. Fill the water bath with water. Set your sous vide machine temperature to 145°F.
4. Rub the beef medallions all over with the spice rub. Place the medallions side by side in food-safe bags and vacuum seal the bags. Use multiple bags if necessary.
5. Place the bags in the water bath and cook sous vide for 12–18 hours.
6. Put the garlic, onion, red pepper, jalapeño, and cilantro stems in a food processor or blender. Process until it is a smooth purée. Add the canned diced tomatoes and pulse a few times.
7. During the last 30 minutes of cooking the roast, heat 2 tablespoons of the oil in a large pot or Dutch oven over medium-high heat. Add the chorizo and cook it through, crumbling it with a wooden spoon, about 8–10 minutes.
8. Stir in the puréed vegetables, wine, lime juice, and orange juice. Bring to a boil and then lower the heat to a simmer. Let the mixture cook for 15–20 minutes or until the liquid reduces and the sauce thickens. Stir in the minced cilantro.
9. Heat 2 tablespoons of the oil in a medium skillet over medium-high heat. Add enough of the plantain slices to cover the bottom of the skillet. Cook until starting to brown, about 2–3 minutes. Flip the plantains and cook until browned on the other side. Drain them on a paper towel. Fry the remaining plantains.

10. Remove the beef slices from the bags and pat dry with a paper towel.
11. Heat the remaining tablespoon of oil in a large skillet over high heat. Sear the beef in the skillet for about 45–60 seconds per side.
12. Remove the beef from the skillet. Let rest for 3–4 minutes.
13. To serve, place the beef medallions on plates and top each with some of the chorizo tomato sauce and a few fried plantains.

Chapter 10
Pork

Korean Pork Ribs

These Asian-style back ribs are "fall off the bone" delicious. Put them in the sous vide before bed and they are ready for dinner the next day!

Ingredients
Serves 2–3

1 rack pork back ribs (around 2 pounds)

½ cup soy sauce

⅓ cup hoisin sauce

¼ packed cup light brown sugar

2 tablespoons sesame oil
2 tablespoons grated fresh gingerroot
2 tablespoons sriracha sauce
3 tablespoons toasted sesame seeds
6 green onions, thinly sliced

1. Peel the thin membrane off the back of the ribs. Cut them into individual rib portions.
2. Make the marinade by whisking together the soy sauce, hoisin sauce, brown sugar, sesame oil, ginger, and sriracha sauce in a medium bowl. Measure out ½ cup marinade sauce, cover, and place in the fridge.
3. Place the ribs in a large bowl and pour the remaining marinade over them. Toss the ribs to ensure they are completely coated in the marinade.

4. Fill the water bath with water. Set your sous vide machine temperature to 176°F.
5. Place the ribs and marinade in a food-safe bag and vacuum seal the bag. Make sure they are lined up side by side and not stacked or piled. Use multiple bags if necessary.
6. Place the ribs in the water bath and cook sous vide for 12–18 hours.
7. Preheat oven to 400°F.
8. Remove the ribs from the water bath. Cut open the bags and use tongs to remove the ribs. Pat them dry with a paper towel and place them on a broiling pan. Brush the ribs with the reserved marinade sauce.
9. Put ribs in the oven and cook for about 6–8 minutes or until the sauce starts to caramelize.
10. Place the ribs on a serving platter and garnish with sesame seeds and green onions.

Korean Pork Ribs

Barbecue Pork Ribs

Do not let the simplicity of this recipe fool you! Use your favorite barbecue sauce and these ribs will rival any that are made on the grill.

Ingredients
Serves 2–3

1 rack pork back ribs (around 2 pounds)

1½ cups barbecue sauce, divided

⅓ packed cup light brown sugar

2 tablespoons Worcestershire sauce

> **Bring the Smoke!**
>
> To simulate ribs made in a backyard smoker, add a few drops of liquid smoke to the bag before sealing. Or, simply use a smoky-flavored sauce like a hickory barbecue sauce to produce great results.

1. Peel the thin membrane off the back of the ribs and cut them into individual rib portions.
2. Make the marinade by whisking together 1 cup of the barbecue sauce with the brown sugar and Worcestershire sauce in a medium bowl.
3. Place the ribs in a large bowl and pour the marinade over them. Toss the ribs to ensure they are completely coated in the marinade.
4. Fill the water bath with water. Set your sous vide machine temperature to 176°F.

5. Place the ribs in a food-safe bag and vacuum seal the bag. Make sure they are lined up side by side and not stacked or piled. Use multiple bags if necessary.
6. Place the ribs in the water bath and cook sous vide for 12–18 hours.
7. Preheat the oven to 400°F.
8. Remove the pouches of ribs from the water bath. Cut open the bags and, using tongs, take out the ribs and place them on a broiling pan. Brush the ribs with the remaining barbecue sauce.
9. Put ribs in the oven and cook for about 6–8 minutes or until the sauce starts to caramelize.

Barbecue Pork Ribs

Honey Garlic Pork Ribs

These ribs have an awesome glaze on them and they are lip-smacking delicious.

Ingredients
Serves 2–3

3 tablespoons butter
8–10 cloves garlic, minced

⅓ cup light soy sauce
1 cup honey
1 rack pork back ribs (around 2 pounds)

Out of the Jar

While this recipe uses a homemade honey garlic sauce, it can turn out just as tasty with a jar of store-bought sauce—and that can make this recipe ridiculously easy to throw together.

---

1. To make the honey garlic sauce, melt the butter in a small saucepan over medium heat. Add the minced garlic and cook for a few minutes to release the flavor, about 2–3 minutes. Add the soy sauce and honey and bring to a boil. Lower the heat to a simmer. The sauce will thicken after 10 minutes or so.

   Measure out ½ cup honey garlic sauce, cover, and place in the fridge.
2. Peel the thin membrane off the back of the ribs and cut them into individual rib portions.
3. Place the ribs in a large bowl and pour the remaining honey garlic sauce on them. Toss the ribs to ensure they are

completely coated in the sauce.
4. Fill the water bath with water. Set your sous vide machine temperature to 176°F.
5. Place the ribs in a food-safe bag and vacuum seal the bag. Make sure they are lined up side by side and not stacked or piled. Use multiple bags if necessary.
6. Place the ribs in the water bath and cook sous vide for 12–18 hours.
7. Preheat the oven to 400°F. Remove the pouches of ribs from the water bath. Cut open the bags and, using tongs, take out the ribs and place them on a broiling pan. Brush the ribs with the reserved honey garlic sauce.
8. Put ribs in the oven and cook for about 6–8 minutes or until the sauce starts to caramelize.

Orange Hoisin Pork Chops

These pork chops are gently cooked in the sous vide water bath so they remain moist and tender. The marinade gives the meat a wonderful sweet citrus taste with an Asian flair.

Ingredients
Serves 4

⅓ cup hoisin sauce

¼ cup freshly squeezed orange juice

2 tablespoons soy sauce

2 tablespoons honey

1 tablespoon sesame oil

1 teaspoon sriracha sauce

1 clove garlic, minced

4 boneless pork loin chops, 1" thick

1 tablespoon oil with a high smoke point, divided (like peanut, sunflower, corn, vegetable, or safflower oil)

1. Make the marinade in a medium bowl by mixing together the hoisin sauce, orange juice, soy sauce, honey, sesame oil, sriracha sauce, and garlic.
2. Fill the water bath with water. Set your sous vide machine temperature to 140°F.
3. Place the pork chops in a food-safe bag and vacuum seal the bag. Make sure the chops are lined up side by side and not stacked or piled. Use multiple bags if necessary.
4. Place the pork in the water bath and cook sous vide for 2 hours.

5. Cut open the bags and, using tongs, remove the pork chops from the bag. Pat them dry with a paper towel.
6. Place the oil in a large skillet over high heat. Sear the pork chops in the skillet for about 45–60 seconds per side.

Thai Pork Chops with Green Curry Sauce

The rich Thai curry sauce is perfectly complemented by the bright flavors of the fresh tomatoes and basil.

Ingredients
Serves 4

¼ cup vegetable oil

2 tablespoons grated fresh gingerroot

2 medium green Thai chilies, minced

1 teaspoon sea salt

4 boneless pork loin chops, 1" thick

1 (14-ounce) can coconut milk

3 tablespoons green curry paste

2 medium tomatoes, diced

¼ cup minced fresh Thai basil

1 tablespoon oil with a high smoke point, divided (like peanut, sunflower, corn, vegetable, or safflower oil)

> **Change the Color**
>
> Thai chili paste comes in green, red, and yellow, with each using different ingredients. Switch things up by using a different curry paste to get a different flavor of sauce. Green curry paste is made with fresh cilantro, kaffir lime leaves, and green Thai chilies. Red curry paste is made with red Thai chilies, tomato paste, and chili powder, while yellow curry paste includes yellow Thai chilies, turmeric, tomato paste, and cumin.

1. Make the marinade by mixing together the oil, ginger, chili peppers, and salt in a medium bowl.

2. Fill the water bath with water. Set your sous vide machine temperature to 140°F.
3. Place the pork chops and the marinade in a food-safe bag and vacuum seal the bag. Make sure the chops are lined up side by side and not stacked or piled. Use multiple bags if necessary.
4. Place the pork in the water bath and cook sous vide for 2 hours.
5. Prior to searing the pork chops, make the green curry sauce. Place the coconut milk and green curry paste in a small saucepan. Heat over medium-high heat until just before boiling, then reduce the heat to low and let the sauce simmer for about 10 minutes.
6. In a small bowl, mix the diced tomatoes with the minced basil.
7. Remove the pork chops from the bag, pat dry with a paper towel. Place the oil in a large skillet over high heat. Sear the pork chops in the skillet for about 45–60 seconds per side.
8. To serve, place each seared pork chop on a plate. Spoon some of the tomato and basil mixture on the chops and pour some green curry sauce on top.

Thai Pork Chops with Green Curry Sauce

24-Hour Sous Vide Pork Belly

Even though this recipe takes a good few days to prepare, it is totally worth it. Sous vide pork belly is incredibly tender and can be used in many different dishes from udon soup to appetizers.

Ingredients
Serves 4–6

1 pork belly slab, about 2 pounds, 2" thick
3 tablespoons sea salt
3 tablespoons soy sauce

¼ cup white sugar
2 tablespoons rice vinegar
1 tablespoon rice wine
2 tablespoons grated fresh gingerroot
2 teaspoons dried red pepper flakes
1 tablespoon vegetable oil

> **Storing Options**
>
> If using this pork belly for another recipe in this book or some other dish, skip the last step. For freezing, cut the pork belly into desired portion sizes and vacuum seal.

1. Rub the pork belly with the salt, cover with plastic wrap, and place in the fridge for 12 hours.
2. Make the marinade by whisking together the remaining ingredients except the oil.
3. Fill the water bath with water. Set your sous vide machine temperature to 176°F.

4. Rinse the pork belly thoroughly and slide into a food-safe bag. Pour in the marinade and vacuum seal the bag. Turn the bag around so the pork belly is completely coated in the marinade.
5. Place the pork belly in the water bath and cook sous vide for 24 hours.
6. Take the bag out of the water and quick chill the pork in ice water. Place in the fridge for 12 hours with a heavy weight on top.
7. Preheat the oven to 325°F. Cut the pork into 2" slices and then cut each slice into 2" segments. Heat an ovenproof skillet over medium heat. Add the oil. Place the pork belly skin side down in the skillet. Fry it for a few minutes to crisp the skin. Place in the oven and bake for 12–15 minutes, until heated through.

Curried Pork Tenderloin with Mint Yogurt Sauce

Pork tenderloin comes out of the sous vide water bath so tender that it basically melts in your mouth. The curry seasoning is mild and is wonderfully complemented by the yogurt sauce.

Ingredients
Serves 4

- 1 cup plain yogurt
- 2 tablespoons minced fresh mint
- 2 tablespoons honey
- 2 tablespoons curry powder
- 1 tablespoon granulated sugar
- 1 teaspoon sea salt
- 2 pork tenderloins (1 pound each)

1. In a small bowl, mix together the yogurt, mint, and honey. Cover with plastic wrap and place in the fridge until serving time.
2. Make the rub by mixing together the curry powder, sugar, and salt in a small bowl. Rub the spice blend all over both tenderloins.
3. Fill the water bath with water. Set your sous vide machine temperature to 140°F.
4. Place the pork tenderloins in separate food-safe bags and vacuum seal the bags.
5. Place the pork in the water bath and cook sous vide for 3 hours.

6. Remove the pork tenderloins from the bag, pat dry with a paper towel, and sear them for about 45–60 seconds per side.
7. Slice into ½" medallions and serve with the mint yogurt sauce.

Curried Pork Tenderloin with Mint Yogurt Sauce

Herb and Garlic Pork Tenderloin with Rose Sauce and Gnocchi

This recipe is a restaurant-quality dish and one that you will be sure to remember. The medallions of pork tenderloin go very well with the gnocchi and rose sauce.

Ingredients
Serves 4

2 tablespoons dried oregano
1 teaspoon garlic powder

½ teaspoon sea salt

½ teaspoon freshly ground black pepper

2 pork tenderloins (approximately 2 pounds each)
4 cups marinara sauce
1 cup heavy cream

½ cup grated Parmesan cheese

2 pounds gnocchi

1. Make the rub by mixing together the oregano, garlic powder, salt, and pepper in a small bowl. Rub the spice blend all over both tenderloins.
2. Fill the water bath with water. Set your sous vide machine temperature to 140°F.
3. Place the pork tenderloins in separate food-safe bags and vacuum seal the bags.
4. Place the pork in the water bath and cook sous vide for 3 hours.

5. Heat the marinara sauce in a large saucepan over medium heat. Let the sauce simmer for 10 minutes. Whisk in the cream and Parmesan cheese. Reduce heat to low.
6. Cook the gnocchi according to the directions on the package. Drain. Pour ¾ of the sauce over the gnocchi and toss until evenly coated.
7. Remove the pork tenderloins from the bag, pat dry with a paper towel, and sear them for about 45–60 seconds per side. Slice them into ½" medallions.
8. To serve, spoon some of the gnocchi on each plate. Place some pork medallions on the gnocchi and pour some of the remaining sauce on the pork.

Pork Carnitas with Pico de Gallo

Carnitas are essentially the Mexican take on pulled pork. The sous vide water bath is an ideal way to cook the pork roast so that the meat is both packed with flavor and easy to shred.

Ingredients
Serves 4–6

- 1 boneless pork butt or shoulder roast (about 4–5 pounds)
- 1 tablespoon vegetable oil
- 1 tablespoon dried oregano
- 1½ teaspoons ground cumin
- ½ teaspoon ground cinnamon
- ¼ teaspoon cayenne pepper
- 1½ teaspoons sea salt
- 1 medium white onion, diced
- 2 navel oranges, peeled and cut into small pieces
- 3 medium tomatoes, diced
- 1 medium sweet onion, finely diced
- ⅓ cup minced fresh cilantro
- 2 medium limes, juiced
- 12 (8") soft flour tortillas
- 2 medium ripe avocados, peeled, pitted, and sliced
- 1 cup grated Oaxaca or Monterey jack cheese

Pico de Gallo?

This is essentially a fresh salsa that is excellent when used as a topping for tacos, fajitas, and more. It is also great scooped up with tortilla chips.

1. Cut the pork roast into 1" cubes.
2. Make the marinade by mixing together the oil, oregano, cumin, cinnamon, cayenne pepper, salt, white onion, and orange in a large bowl. Toss the cubed pork in the marinade until the pieces are evenly coated.
3. Fill the water bath with water. Set your sous vide machine temperature to 176°F.
4. Place the pork in a food-safe bag and vacuum seal the bag. Make sure the cubes are lined up side by side and not stacked or piled. Use multiple bags if necessary.
5. Place the pork in the water bath and cook sous vide for 12–18 hours.
6. Remove the pork from the bags and drain. Once cool enough to handle, use a fork to shred the meat.
7. Make the pico de gallo by mixing together the diced tomatoes, sweet onion, cilantro, and lime juice.
8. Preheat the oven to broil. Spread out the shredded meat on a baking sheet and cook in the oven until starting to crisp, about 5–8 minutes.
9. Assemble the carnitas by placing some meat on each tortilla. Top with pico de gallo, avocado, and grated cheese.

Barbecue Pulled Pork

Tender, juicy, and full of flavor, this pulled pork recipe is great on a bun with lots of barbecue sauce and topped with coleslaw.

Ingredients
Serves 4–6

1 boneless pork butt or shoulder roast (about 4–5 pounds)
1 tablespoon vegetable oil
1 packed tablespoon light brown sugar
1 tablespoon paprika

1½ teaspoons sea salt

1 teaspoon ground cumin
1 teaspoon freshly ground black pepper

½ teaspoon dried oregano

¼ teaspoon cayenne pepper

2 cups barbecue sauce

Use in Many Other Recipes

Pulled pork is so delicious that one bite will get you thinking about the many things that this pork can be used for. Top a pizza or nachos with some of the pulled pork, or use it in shepherd's pie, wraps, and more!

---

1. Cut the pork roast into 1" cubes.
2. Make the barbecue rub by mixing together the oil, brown sugar, paprika, salt, cumin, black pepper, oregano, and cayenne pepper in a large bowl. Toss the cubed pork in the rub until evenly coated.

3. Fill the water bath with water. Set your sous vide machine temperature to 176°F.
4. Place the pork in a food-safe bag and vacuum seal the bag. Make sure the cubes are lined up side by side and not stacked or piled. Use multiple bags if necessary.
5. Place the pork in the water bath and cook sous vide for 12–18 hours.
6. Remove the pork from the bag and drain. Once cool enough to handle, use a fork to shred the meat. Pour in the barbecue sauce and mix until the meat is evenly coated in sauce.
7. Serve the pulled pork on fresh kaiser rolls with coleslaw.

Barbecue Pulled Pork

Pulled Pork Shepherd's Pie

For anyone who thought that shepherd's pie is boring, they never tried this recipe! The pulled pork gives this comfort food an upgrade and has an awesome barbecue flavor.

Ingredients
Serves 4–6

5–6 cups *Barbecue Pulled Pork* (see recipe in this chapter)
1 cup frozen peas
1 cup frozen corn
3–4 cups sous vide *Mashed Potatoes* (see recipe in Chapter 13)
1½ cups grated Cheddar cheese

1. Preheat the oven to 350°F.
2. Spread pulled pork on the bottom of a 13" × 9" baking dish.
3. Sprinkle frozen peas and corn on top of the pork.
4. Spread the mashed potatoes on top of the frozen veggies.
5. Top with the grated cheese.
6. Bake in the oven for 45–60 minutes. The cheese should be starting to brown and some barbecue sauce should be bubbling up the sides.

Pulled Pork Shepherd's Pie

Asian Pork Lettuce Wraps

These pork lettuce wraps are a healthy treat.

Ingredients
Serves 4–6

1 boneless pork butt or shoulder roast (about 3–4 pounds)
1 tablespoon vegetable oil
5 tablespoons soy sauce, divided
2 tablespoons fresh grated ginger
3 garlic cloves, minced
3 tablespoons packed brown sugar
3 tablespoons rice vinegar

1½ tablespoons sesame oil

1½ tablespoons sriracha sauce
3 tablespoons sugar
3 cups cooked rice (long grain, jasmine, or other)
1 head Boston lettuce
4 green onions, sliced

1. Cut the pork roast into 1" cubes.
2. Make the marinade by mixing together the vegetable oil, 2 tablespoons soy sauce, grated ginger, minced garlic, and brown sugar in a large bowl. Toss the cubed pork in the marinade until the pieces are evenly coated.
3. Fill the water bath with water. Set your sous vide machine temperature to 170°F.
4. Place the pork in a food-safe bag and vacuum seal the bag. Make sure the cubes are lined up side by side and not stacked

or piled. Use multiple bags if necessary.
5. Place the pork in the water bath and cook sous vide for 12–18 hours.
6. Make the sauce by whisking together the remaining soy sauce, rice vinegar, sesame oil, sriracha sauce, and sugar, until the sugar is dissolved.
7. Remove the pork from the bags and drain. Once cool enough to handle, use a fork to shred the meat.
8. Assemble the lettuce wraps by placing some rice on a Boston lettuce leaf. Add some pork and top with some sliced green onions. Drizzle some of the sauce on top of the meat and rice.

Chapter 11
Seafood

Korean Shrimp

This shrimp dish has a wonderful Asian flavor that is distinctly Korean, with the perfect combination of sweet, heat, and sour.

Ingredients
Serves 4

3 tablespoons gochujang (fermented hot pepper paste)
3 tablespoons granulated sugar
2 tablespoons rice vinegar
2 tablespoons soy sauce
2 tablespoons sesame oil
1 pound raw medium shrimp, peeled and deveined

Don't Waste That Sauce!

The sauce in this shrimp recipe is so delicious that it almost seems wrong to just eat the shrimp individually and waste the sauce. Turn this dish into a full meal by tossing the shrimp and sauce with some steamed or stir-fried vegetables and then serve it over a bed of rice. Just amazing!

---

1. Make the marinade by mixing together the gochujang, sugar, rice vinegar, soy sauce, and sesame oil in a medium bowl. Toss the shrimp in the marinade.
2. Fill the water bath with water. Set your sous vide machine temperature to 140°F.
3. Dump the coated shrimp and the marinade in a food-safe bag and vacuum seal the bag. Make sure the shrimp are lined up side by side and not stacked or piled. Use multiple bags if necessary.

4. Place the shrimp in the water bath and cook sous vide for 30 minutes.
5. Pour the shrimp and sauce into a large bowl and serve immediately.

Garlic Butter Shrimp

These buttery shrimp are so tasty that you may find yourself needing to make another batch for the guests! Serve with pasta or rice to make a filling and delicious dish.

Ingredients
Serves 4

- 3 tablespoons butter, melted
- 2 teaspoons garlic powder
- 1 teaspoon sea salt
- 1 pound raw medium shrimp, peeled and deveined

> **Don't Overcook the Shrimp**
>
> One of the significant benefits of sous vide cooking is that it is extremely forgiving in regards to overcooking meat. While beef, chicken, pork, and many other meats can be in the sous vide water bath far longer than the length it takes to cook the food, shrimp on the other hand, is more delicate and needs to be removed once it has been cooked for 30 minutes. Any longer and the texture of the shrimp will be negatively affected.

1. Make the garlic butter by mixing together the melted butter, garlic powder, and salt in a medium bowl. Toss the shrimp in the garlic butter.
2. Fill the water bath with water. Set your sous vide machine temperature to 140°F.
3. Pour the coated shrimp and the garlic butter in a food-safe bag and vacuum seal the bag. Make sure the shrimp are lined up side by side and not stacked or piled. Use multiple bags if necessary.

4. Place the shrimp in the water bath and cook sous vide for 30 minutes.
5. Pour the shrimp and sauce into a large bowl and serve immediately.

Pasta with Shrimp and Roasted Red Pepper Cream Sauce

This dish of succulent shrimp with a creamy cheese sauce is worthy of being a dinner party entrée.

Ingredients
Serves 4

- 1 pound raw medium shrimp, peeled and deveined
- ¼ cup butter
- ½ red onion, minced
- 4 cloves garlic, minced
- 1½ cups heavy cream
- 1 cup cream cheese
- ½ cup grated Parmesan cheese
- 5 jarred roasted red peppers, diced
- 1 teaspoon sea salt
- 1 teaspoon freshly ground black pepper
- 16 ounces dry pasta (penne, farfalle, rotini, etc.)
- ⅓ cup torn fresh basil

1. Fill the water bath with water. Set your sous vide machine temperature to 140°F.
2. Place the shrimp in a food-safe bag and vacuum seal the bag. Make sure the shrimp are lined up side by side and not stacked or piled. Use multiple bags if necessary.

3. Place the shrimp in the water bath and cook sous vide for 30 minutes.
4. Meanwhile, in a medium saucepan, melt butter over medium heat. Add the red onion and garlic and cook until tender, about 5 minutes. Stir in the heavy cream, cream cheese, Parmesan cheese, and roasted red peppers. Stir until the cream cheese melts into the sauce. Keep the sauce at a medium-low simmer so that it doesn't come to a boil. Stir in the salt and pepper.
5. Cook the pasta according to directions on the package. Drain.
6. Take the shrimp out of the water bath and drain them of any liquid that was in the bag.
7. Toss the pasta in the sauce with the shrimp. Top with fresh basil.

Shrimp Creole

This classic dish from southern Louisiana has hints of Spanish and French cuisine. By cooking the shrimp sous vide, it ensures that they are perfectly cooked for this delicious dish.

Ingredients
Serves 4

1 pound raw medium shrimp, peeled and deveined

1½ teaspoons creole seasoning

3 tablespoons vegetable oil
1 medium yellow onion, diced
1 medium green bell pepper, cored and diced
3 stalks celery, diced
4 cloves garlic, minced
1 (28-ounce) can diced tomatoes
1 teaspoon sea salt
1 teaspoon freshly ground black pepper
1 teaspoon dried oregano

½ teaspoon dried thyme

½ teaspoon ground white pepper

½ teaspoon cayenne pepper
6–8 cups cooked long-grain white rice

1. Fill the water bath with water. Set your sous vide machine temperature to 140°F.
2. Toss shrimp in the creole seasoning. Place the shrimp in a food-safe bag and vacuum seal the bag. Make sure the shrimp

are lined up side by side and not stacked or piled. Use multiple bags if necessary.
3. Place the shrimp in the water bath and cook sous vide for 30 minutes.
4. Meanwhile, in a medium saucepan, heat the oil over medium heat. Add the onion, green pepper, celery, and garlic and cook until tender, about 5–7 minutes. Stir in the diced tomatoes, salt, black pepper, oregano, thyme, white pepper, and cayenne pepper. Bring to a boil and lower heat to a simmer. Cook for 20–30 minutes.
5. Take the shrimp out of the water bath and drain them of any liquid that was in the bag.
6. To serve, spoon some of the tomato mixture on a bed of rice and top with some shrimp.

Salmon with Edamame and Corn Succotash

If anyone has ever said that healthy food does not taste good, then they have never tried this recipe. Packed with flavor, this dish is also packed with health!

Ingredients
Serves 4

½ cup kosher salt

8 cups water

4 cups ice cubes

4 (4–6-ounce) fresh salmon fillets, 1" thick, skin removed

¼ cup olive oil, divided

1 medium red onion, diced

1 medium red bell pepper, cored and diced

2 cloves garlic, minced

3 cups frozen corn

3 cups shelled edamame

2 teaspoons sea salt

1 teaspoon freshly ground black pepper

3 tablespoons minced fresh flat-leaf parsley

Salmon Cooking Temperature

People have very different preferences when it comes to the doneness of salmon. This recipe sets the temperature of the water at 126°F, which cooks the salmon to be a little on the firm side but still very moist. For a salmon that has a texture closer to a traditional cooking method, cook at 140°F. In all cases, the cook time is the same at 30 minutes.

1. Prepare the brine by dumping the kosher salt, water, and ice cubes in a large container. Stir until the salt is dissolved. Add the salmon and cover the container with plastic wrap. Place in the fridge and brine for 20–60 minutes.
2. Fill the water bath with water. Set your sous vide machine temperature to 126°F.
3. Drain the salmon and rinse thoroughly in cold water.
4. Place the salmon fillets and 2 tablespoons of the olive oil in a food-safe bag and vacuum seal the bag. Make sure the salmon is lined up side by side and not stacked or piled. Use multiple bags if necessary.
5. Place the salmon in the water bath and cook sous vide for 30 minutes.
6. Make the succotash by heating the remaining olive oil in a medium skillet over medium heat. Add the red onion, red bell pepper, and garlic and cook until tender, about 5 minutes. Add the corn and edamame and cook for another 8–10 minutes, stirring often. Add salt, pepper, and fresh parsley. Stir and remove from the heat.
7. Remove the salmon from the water bath.
8. To serve, place a fillet of salmon on each plate and spoon some edamame and corn succotash over the salmon.

Salmon with Orange Butter Sauce and Pickled Fennel

The salmon is delicately cooked and complemented by the creamy sauce and the tang of the pickled fennel.

Ingredients
Serves 4

½ cup kosher salt

8 cups water

4 cups ice cubes

4 (4–6-ounce) fresh salmon fillets, 1" thick, skin removed

2 tablespoons olive oil

⅔ cup orange juice

¼ cup dry white wine

2 medium shallots, minced

1 teaspoon sea salt

½ cup heavy cream

¾ cup butter, cut into small cubes

1 cup *Spicy Pickled Fennel* (see recipe in Chapter 15)

Brining the Salmon

While brining is not necessary, it does have some significant benefits to cooking salmon. Brining removes excess water from the salmon and enhances the texture of the fish. It also helps retain the deep color of the salmon, which usually goes pale pink during cooking. Finally, brining helps prevent the white "film" from coming out of the salmon while it is cooked.

1. Prepare the brine by dumping the kosher salt, water, and ice cubes in a large container. Stir until the salt is dissolved. Add the salmon and cover the container with plastic wrap. Place in the fridge and brine for 20–60 minutes.
2. Fill the water bath with water. Set your sous vide machine temperature to 126°F.
3. Drain the salmon and rinse thoroughly in cold water.
4. Place the salmon fillets and olive oil in a food-safe bag and vacuum seal the bag. Make sure the salmon is lined up side by side and not stacked or piled. Use multiple bags if necessary.
5. Place the salmon in the water bath and cook sous vide for 30 minutes.
6. Make the orange butter sauce by adding the orange juice, white wine, shallots, and salt to a medium saucepan. Bring to a boil and then reduce the heat. Let the sauce simmer for 5–7 minutes, until the shallots are tender and the liquid reduces by about one third. Pour in the heavy cream and let the sauce simmer for another 5 minutes. Add the cubed butter and whisk continually until all the butter is melted and emulsified into the sauce. Remove from the heat.
7. Remove the salmon from the water bath.
8. To serve, pour some orange butter sauce on a plate and place the salmon in the center of the sauce. Spoon some of the Spicy Pickled Fennel on top of the salmon.

Salmon with Sun-Dried Tomato Basil Compound Butter

This recipe is all about simplicity, and the rich compound butter perfectly accentuates the delicate taste of the salmon.

Ingredients
Serves 4

½ cup kosher salt

8 cups water

4 cups ice cubes

4 (4–6-ounce) fresh salmon fillets, 1" thick, skin removed

2 tablespoons olive oil

½ cup salted butter, softened

3 oil-packed sun-dried tomatoes, drained and minced

1 teaspoon minced fresh oregano

2 teaspoons minced fresh flat-leaf parsley

1 tablespoon oil with a high smoke point (like peanut, sunflower, corn, vegetable, or safflower oil)

1 teaspoon sea salt

½ teaspoon freshly ground black pepper

Searing the Salmon

Sous vide salmon is light, flaky, and extremely delicate. Searing one side in some hot oil provides a crispy contrast to the soft and tender texture of the fish. Searing salmon is quick; about 1 minute is sufficient. Season the fish by sprinkling some sea salt and freshly ground black pepper on the seared side.

1. Prepare the brine by dumping the kosher salt, water, and ice cubes in a large container. Stir until the salt is dissolved. Add the salmon and cover the container with plastic wrap. Place in the fridge and brine for 20–60 minutes.
2. Fill the water bath with water. Set your sous vide machine temperature to 126°F.
3. Drain the salmon and rinse thoroughly in cold water.
4. Place the salmon fillets and the olive oil in a food-safe bag and vacuum seal the bag. Make sure the salmon is lined up side by side and not stacked or piled. Use multiple bags if necessary.
5. Place the salmon in the water bath and cook sous vide for 30 minutes.
6. Make the compound butter by mixing together the softened butter, sun-dried tomatoes, oregano, and parsley. Form the butter into a long cylinder that is about 1½" in diameter. Roll the butter in plastic wrap and twist the ends. Place in the fridge to allow the butter to harden.
7. Remove the salmon from the bag and pat dry with a paper towel.
8. Heat the oil in a large skillet over high heat. Sear the salmon in the skillet on one side for only about 1 minute.
9. Remove the salmon from the skillet and sprinkle the seared side with the sea salt and black pepper.
10. Take the compound butter out of the fridge and remove the plastic wrap. Slice the butter into ¼–1/2" rounds.
11. To serve, place a salmon fillet seared-side down on each dinner plate and top with 2–3 slices of the compound butter.

No-Fuss Scallops

Sous vide takes away any of the difficulty in cooking scallops and this recipe has them fully cooked right through and pan-seared on the outside. Divine!

Ingredients
Serves 4

- 12 large sea scallops
- 1 tablespoon oil with a high smoke point (like peanut, sunflower, corn, vegetable, or safflower oil)
- 1 teaspoon sea salt
- ½ teaspoon freshly ground black pepper

Make It a Meal

Turn these scallops into a meal by serving them alongside some of the recipes in Chapter 13. Top the *Risotto with Parmesan and Peas* with a few of these sous vide scallops for a rich, hearty dinner. Or go light by serving the scallops with some of the *Maple Butternut Squash Purée*.

---

1. Fill the water bath with water. Set your sous vide machine temperature to 140°F.
2. Place the scallops in a food-safe bag and vacuum seal the bag. Make sure the scallops are lined up side by side and not stacked or piled. Use multiple bags if necessary.
3. Place the scallops in the water bath and cook sous vide for 40 minutes.
4. Remove the scallops from the bag and pat dry with a paper towel.

5. Heat the oil in a large skillet on high heat. Sear the scallops in the skillet for about 30–45 seconds per side.
6. Remove the scallops from the skillet and sprinkle with salt and pepper.

Jerk Fish Tacos with Pineapple Coconut Salsa

These tacos have a taste like they are right from the Caribbean. The fish has that island jerk flavor and the salsa is bright and fruity.

Ingredients
Serves 4

1–2 teaspoons jerk seasoning
4 (4–6-ounce) fish fillets (sea bass, mahi-mahi, or halibut), 1" thick
2 cups cubed fresh pineapple

⅔ cup shaved fresh coconut

2 medium jalapeño peppers, cored and minced
2 tablespoons minced fresh mint
2 tablespoons lime juice
1 tablespoon olive oil
2 tablespoons honey
8–12 (6") soft flour tortillas

1. Fill the water bath with water. Set your sous vide machine temperature to 135°F.
2. Rub the jerk seasoning all over the fish.
3. Place the fillets in a food-safe bag and vacuum seal the bag. Make sure the fish is lined up side by side and not stacked or piled. Use multiple bags if necessary.
4. Place the fish in the water bath and cook sous vide for 45 minutes.
5. Make the salsa by tossing the pineapple, coconut, jalapeño peppers, and mint in a medium bowl. In a small bowl, whisk

together the lime juice, olive oil, and honey. Pour the liquid mixture over the salsa and stir until combined.
6. Remove the fish from the bag and crumble.
7. Assemble the tacos by placing some of the crumbled fish on each soft tortilla. Spoon some of the pineapple coconut salsa on top.

Mahi-Mahi with Blush Sauce and Pasta

This blush sauce is surprisingly light and perfect to go alongside the delicate flavor of the mahi-mahi.

Ingredients
Serves 4

4 (4–6-ounce) mahi-mahi fish fillets, 1" thick
2 tablespoons butter
1 medium sweet onion, minced

½ medium yellow bell pepper, cored and diced

2 cloves garlic, minced
1 (28-ounce) can diced tomatoes
1 cup heavy cream

⅓ cup grated Parmesan cheese

1 teaspoon sea salt

½ teaspoon freshly ground black pepper

16 ounces dry pasta (penne, farfalle, rotini, etc.)

¼ cup minced fresh flat-leaf parsley

1. Fill the water bath with water. Set your sous vide machine temperature to 135°F.
2. Place the mahi-mahi fillets in a food-safe bag and vacuum seal the bag. Make sure the fish is lined up side by side and not stacked or piled. Use multiple bags if necessary.
3. Place the mahi-mahi in the water bath and cook sous vide for 45 minutes.

4. In a medium saucepan, melt the butter over medium heat. Add the onion, bell pepper, and garlic and cook until tender, about 5 minutes. Add the diced tomatoes and bring to a boil. Reduce the heat to low and let the sauce simmer for about 10 minutes. Stir in the heavy cream and Parmesan cheese. Keep the sauce at a medium-low simmer so that it doesn't come to a boil. Stir in the salt and pepper.
5. Cook the pasta according to the directions on the package. Drain.
6. Take the mahi-mahi out of the water bath and drain them of any liquid that was in the bag.
7. Toss the pasta in ⅔ of the sauce. To serve, spoon some of the pasta on each plate. Place a mahi-mahi fillet on top of the pasta and spoon some of the remaining blush sauce on top of the mahi-mahi. Sprinkle some fresh parsley on top.

Mahi-Mahi with Peach and Mango Chutney

This ocean fish goes great with tropical flavors and this fruity chutney is the perfect topping.

Ingredients
Serves 4

4 (4–6-ounce) mahi-mahi fish fillets, 1" thick
1 teaspoon sea salt

½ teaspoon freshly ground black pepper

2 cups *Peach and Mango Chutney* (see recipe in Chapter 15)

1. Fill the water bath with water. Set your sous vide machine temperature to 135°F.
2. Place the mahi-mahi fillets in a food-safe bag and vacuum seal the bag. Make sure the fish is lined up side by side and not stacked or piled. Use multiple bags if necessary.
3. Place the mahi-mahi in the water bath and cook sous vide for 45 minutes.
4. Remove the mahi-mahi from the bag and sprinkle with salt and pepper.
5. To serve, place a mahi-mahi fillet on each plate and spoon some Peach and Mango Chutney on top of the fish.

Halibut with Sicilian Ragu

With all the flavors of an Italian coastal dish, the ragu perfectly complements the delicate taste of the halibut.

Ingredients
Serves 4

4 (4–6-ounce) fresh halibut fillets, 1" thick

¼ cup olive oil, divided

1 tablespoon fresh oregano, minced
3 medium shallots, minced
2 cloves garlic, minced
2 cups quartered grape tomatoes
1 cup diced pitted kalamata olives

⅓ cup capers, drained and rinsed

½ cup dry white wine

1 teaspoon sea salt
1 teaspoon freshly ground black pepper

⅓ cup minced fresh basil

1. Fill the water bath with water. Set your sous vide machine temperature to 135°F.
2. Toss the halibut fillets in 2 tablespoons of the oil and the oregano.
3. Place the coated halibut fillets in a food-safe bag and vacuum seal the bag. Make sure the halibut is lined up side by side and not stacked or piled. Use multiple bags if necessary.

4. Place the fish in the water bath and cook sous vide for 45 minutes.
5. Make the ragu by heating the remaining olive oil in a medium skillet over medium heat. Add the shallots, garlic, grape tomatoes, kalamata olives, and capers. Cook until tender, about 5 minutes. Add the white wine, salt, and pepper. Cook for another 3–5 minutes. Remove from the heat and stir in the fresh basil.
6. Remove the halibut from the water bath.
7. To serve, place a halibut fillet on each plate and spoon some Sicilian ragu over the fish.

Chapter 12
Other Meats

Holiday Turkey Breast

Using a sous vide water bath produces a turkey breast that is tender and juicy. It will impress those guests who think that breast meat is always dry and tough.

Ingredients
Serves 2–3

1 teaspoon sea salt
1 teaspoon freshly ground black pepper
1 boneless turkey breast (with skin on), 2" thick, about 2 pounds
2–3 leaves fresh sage
1 sprig fresh thyme

> **Crisp Up That Skin**
>
> If you want some crispy skin, it can be done a couple of different ways. One method is to pat dry the skin with a paper towel. Then place the turkey skin side down in a skillet and sear it over medium-high heat for a few minutes. The other way is to place the turkey skin side up on a baking sheet and put it in the oven on broil for a few minutes until the skin gets crispy.

1. Sprinkle the salt and pepper on the turkey breast.
2. Place the turkey breast, fresh sage, and thyme in a food-safe bag and vacuum seal the bag.
3. Fill the water bath with water. Set your sous vide machine temperature to 146°F.
4. Place the turkey breast in the water bath and cook sous vide for 3–6 hours.
5. Take the turkey out of the bag, peel off the skin, and carve it into ½"-thick slices.

Holiday Turkey Breast (with crispy skin)

Turkey Breast with Pistachio Mushroom Dressing

Instead of stuffing a turkey, cook the turkey breast in the sous vide so that it is tender and juicy while baking the dressing in the oven, making it toasty and delicious.

Ingredients
Serves 4–6

2 teaspoons sea salt
2 teaspoons freshly ground black pepper
2 boneless turkey breasts (with skin on), 2" thick, about 2 pounds for each breast

¼ cup butter
4 medium shallots, minced
5 cups diced button or cremini mushrooms
1 cup salted pistachios
1 cup panko bread crumbs

½ cup grated Parmesan cheese
2 teaspoons minced fresh oregano

1. Sprinkle the salt and pepper on the turkey breasts.
2. Place the turkey breasts in a food-safe bag and vacuum seal the bag. Make sure the breasts are side by side and not stacked. Use multiple bags if necessary.
3. Fill the water bath with water. Set your sous vide machine temperature to 146°F.
4. Place the turkey breasts in the water bath and cook sous vide for 3–6 hours.

5. In a large skillet, melt the butter over medium heat. Add the shallots and mushrooms and sauté until soft and tender, about 4–6 minutes. Remove from the heat and let cool to room temperature.
6. Using a food processor, crush the pistachios. Stop when they are an uneven consistency—some coarse and some fine.
7. In a large bowl, stir together the pistachios, mushroom mixture, panko bread crumbs, Parmesan cheese, and fresh oregano. Pour the stuffing into a medium-sized casserole dish.
8. Preheat the oven to 375°F. About 30 minutes before the turkey breasts are done cooking, place the casserole dish, uncovered, in the oven and bake the dressing for 25–30 minutes. The dressing should be toasty brown.
9. Take the turkey out of the bag, peel off the skin, and carve it into ½"-thick slices.
10. To serve, place a few slices of turkey breast on each plate and spoon some of the dressing next to the turkey.

Turkey Breast with Apple Cranberry Chutney

The sweet and sour chutney makes this recipe ideal for any Christmas or Thanksgiving dinner, and the toasted walnuts are the perfect crunchy addition.

Ingredients
Serves 4–6

- 2 teaspoons sea salt
- 2 teaspoons freshly ground black pepper
- 2 boneless turkey breasts (with skin on), 2" thick, about 2 pounds for each breast
- ½ cup water
- ½ cup apple cider vinegar
- ½ cup granulated sugar
- 1 medium sweet onion, minced
- 4 medium apples, (McIntosh, Gala, etc.) peeled, cored, and diced
- 3 cups fresh or frozen cranberries
- 1 cup roughly chopped toasted walnuts

1. Sprinkle the salt and pepper on the turkey breasts.
2. Place the turkey breasts in a food-safe bag and vacuum seal the bag. Make sure the breasts are side by side and not stacked. Use multiple bags if necessary.
3. Fill the water bath with water. Set your sous vide machine temperature to 146°F.

4. Place the turkey breasts in the water bath and cook sous vide for 3–6 hours.
5. In a medium saucepan make the chutney by bringing the water, cider vinegar, and sugar to a low boil. Whisk until the sugar is dissolved. Add the minced onion. Cook until the onion is tender, about 3–4 minutes. Add the diced apple and cranberries and place the lid on the saucepan. Lower the heat to a simmer and cook until the apples are soft and the cranberries are plump and break, about 8–10 minutes. Remove the lid and continue to simmer, stirring often until the sauce thickens. Remove from the heat.
6. Take the turkey out of the bag, peel off the skin, and carve it into ½"-thick slices.
7. To serve, place a few slices of turkey breast on each plate, spoon some of the chutney on top of the turkey, and sprinkle some chopped walnuts on top.

Succulent Duck Breast

This duck breast is perfectly cooked to a medium-rare and is both moist and tender with a crispy skin.

Ingredients
Serves 1

1 boneless (6–8 ounce) duck breast, with skin on

½ teaspoon sea salt

½ teaspoon freshly ground black pepper

1 tablespoon oil with a high smoke point (like peanut, sunflower, corn, vegetable, or safflower oil)

> **The Easy Way to Cook Duck**
>
> So many people say that cooking duck is difficult because it often comes out overcooked and tough. Using sous vide takes the guess work out of cooking duck and results in a perfectly rare duck breast every time!

1. Fill the water bath with water. Set your sous vide machine temperature to 135°F.
2. Rub the duck breast all over with the salt and pepper. Place the duck in a food-safe bag and vacuum seal the bag.
3. Place the duck in the water bath and cook sous vide for 90 minutes.
4. Remove the duck from the bag and pat dry with a paper towel.
5. Heat the oil in a small skillet over medium heat. Sear the duck in the skillet skin side down for about 3–4 minutes. The skin should be crispy and the fat rendered.
6. Serve immediately.

Duck Breast with Basil Pesto and Pomegranate Reduction

The bright, fresh flavor of pesto is matched by the deep, rich notes of the pomegranate reduction sauce and both are the perfect complement to duck breast.

Ingredients
Serves 4

- 4 boneless (6–8 ounce) duck breasts, with skin on
- ½ teaspoon sea salt
- ½ teaspoon freshly ground black pepper
- 2 cups pomegranate juice
- ¼ cup brandy
- ⅓ cup granulated sugar
- 1⅓ packed cups basil leaves
- 2 cloves garlic
- ½ cup pine nuts
- ⅓ cup grated Parmesan cheese
- ½ cup olive oil
- 1 tablespoon oil with a high smoke point (like peanut, sunflower, corn, vegetable, or safflower oil)
- ⅓ cup pomegranate arils/seeds

Make-Ahead Options

The basil pesto and pomegranate reduction sauce give this recipe a number of steps. To make things a little easier around dinnertime, it is definitely possible to make the pesto and reduction sauce ahead, maybe even the day before. Simply keep them covered and in the fridge, ready for plating once the duck is cooked. Just let the reduction sauce come to room temperature before plating.

1. Fill the water bath with water. Set your sous vide machine temperature to 135°F.
2. Rub the duck breasts all over with the salt and pepper. Place the duck in a food-safe bag and vacuum seal the bag. Make sure the breasts are lined up side by side and not stacked. Use multiple bags if necessary.
3. Place the duck in the water bath and cook sous vide for 90 minutes.
4. Make the pomegranate sauce by adding the pomegranate juice, brandy, and sugar to a medium saucepan. Bring to a boil, and then lower heat to a simmer. Reduce the liquid until there is about ½ cup of sauce. This takes about 30 minutes.
5. Make the pesto by adding the basil, garlic, pine nuts, and Parmesan cheese to a food processor. Turn on the food processor and slowly pour in the olive oil until incorporated and the pesto is fairly smooth.
6. Remove the duck from the bag and pat dry with a paper towel.
7. Heat the 1 tablespoon oil in a large skillet over medium heat. Sear the duck in the skillet skin side down on medium heat for about 3–4 minutes. The skin should be crispy and the fat rendered. Slice the duck breasts.
8. To serve, spread some pesto on each dinner plate. Spread sliced duck on the pesto. Drizzle with pomegranate sauce, sprinkle with pomegranate seeds, and serve immediately.

Duck Breast with Basil Pesto and Pomegranate Reduction

Herb-Infused Lamb Chops

Sometimes simple is best. The fresh herbs in this dish are all that is needed to both highlight the wonderful richness of the lamb chops and give them an enhanced aromatic flavor.

Ingredients
Serves 4

- 8 (3-ounce) lamb loin chops, 1" thick
- 2 sprigs fresh herbs (rosemary, thyme, oregano, tarragon, etc.)
- 1 tablespoon oil with a high smoke point (like peanut, sunflower, corn, vegetable, or safflower oil)
- 2 tablespoons butter
- 1 teaspoon sea salt
- ½ teaspoon freshly ground black pepper

Watch Those Bones

Lamb chops obviously have bones and they can have sharp points that can pierce the bag during the vacuum sealing. One possible solution is to use the pulse feature on the vacuum sealer to control how much air is pulled out of the bag and to stop it just as the bag wraps around the lamb chops. This can get all the air out while stopping it just before the bag gets pierced.

---

1. Fill the water bath with water. Set your sous vide machine temperature to 134°F for medium rare. If a different doneness for lamb is desired, check *Appendix A: Time and Temperature Charts*.
2. Place the lamb chops and sprigs of fresh herbs in a food-safe bag and vacuum seal the bag. Make sure the lamb chops are

lined up side by side and not stacked or piled. Use multiple bags if necessary.
3. Place the lamb chops in the water bath and cook sous vide for 2–4 hours.
4. Remove the lamb chops from the bag and pat dry with a paper towel.
5. Heat the oil in a large skillet over high heat. Sear the lamb chops in the skillet for about 1–2 minutes per side. While the lamb chops are searing, add the butter to the skillet and use a spoon to baste the top of the chops with the melted butter.
6. Remove the lamb chops from the skillet and sprinkle with the salt and pepper.

Herb-Infused Lamb Chops

Lamb Chops with Lemon Mint and Black Olive Butter

This compound butter is filled with delicate flavors that come together perfectly and add so much complexity as the butter melts on the lamb chops.

Ingredients
Serves 4

8 (3-ounce) lamb loin chops, 1" thick

½ cup salted butter, softened

3 tablespoons minced black olives

1 tablespoon minced fresh mint

2 teaspoons lemon juice

1 tablespoon oil with a high smoke point (like peanut, sunflower, corn, vegetable, or safflower oil)

1 teaspoon sea salt

½ teaspoon freshly ground black pepper

1. Fill the water bath with water. Set your sous vide machine temperature to 134°F for medium rare. If a different doneness for lamb is desired, check *Appendix A: Time and Temperature Charts*.
2. Place the lamb chops in a food-safe bag and vacuum seal the bag. Make sure the lamb chops are lined up side by side and not stacked or piled. Use multiple bags if necessary.
3. Place the lamb chops in the water bath and cook sous vide for 2–4 hours.

4. Make the compound butter by mixing together the softened butter, black olives, mint, and lemon juice in a medium bowl.

   Form into a long cylinder that is about 1½" in diameter. Roll up the butter in plastic wrap and twist the ends. Place in the fridge to allow the butter to harden.
5. Remove the lamb chops from the bag and pat dry with a paper towel.
6. Heat the oil in a large skillet over high heat. Sear the lamb chops in the skillet for about 1–2 minutes per side.
7. Remove the lamb chops from the skillet and sprinkle with the salt and pepper.
8. Take the compound butter out of the fridge and remove the plastic wrap. Slice the butter into ¼–1/2" rounds.
9. Put 2 lamb chops on each dinner plate and top each chop with a slice of the compound butter. Serve.

Lamb Chops with Roasted Grapes and Feta

Roasting the grapes sweetens them considerably and they are complemented by the rich sourness of the balsamic vinegar and the saltiness of the feta. All of this works together with the lamb chops for a savory taste experience.

Ingredients
Serves 4

8 (3-ounce) lamb loin chops, 1" thick
2 tablespoons white grape juice
3 cups seedless red grapes
1 tablespoon olive oil
1 tablespoon oil with a high smoke point (like peanut, sunflower, corn, vegetable, or safflower oil)
1 teaspoon sea salt

½ teaspoon freshly ground black pepper

¼ cup balsamic vinegar

⅓ cup crumbled feta cheese

1. Fill the water bath with water. Set your sous vide machine temperature to 134°F for medium rare. If a different doneness for lamb is desired, check *Appendix A: Time and Temperature Charts*.
2. Place the lamb chops and white grape juice in a food-safe bag and vacuum seal the bag. Make sure the lamb chops are lined up side by side and not stacked or piled. Use multiple bags if necessary.

3. Place the lamb chops in the water bath and cook sous vide for 2–4 hours.
4. Preheat the oven to 400°F. Place the grapes on a large baking sheet and drizzle with the olive oil. Place in the oven and roast for 20–30 minutes.
5. Remove the lamb chops from the bag and pat dry with a paper towel.
6. Heat the oil in a large skillet over high heat. Sear the lamb chops in the skillet for about 1–2 minutes per side. Remove the lamb chops from the skillet.
7. Put 2 lamb chops on each dinner plate and surround with roasted grapes. Sprinkle the lamb chops and roasted grapes with the salt and pepper. Drizzle with balsamic vinegar and top with feta cheese. Serve.

Rack of Lamb with Caper Cream Sauce

This rich and creamy sauce with salty capers goes so well with the deep yet delicate taste of lamb.

Ingredients
Serves 4

2 teaspoons dried oregano
1 teaspoon garlic powder
4 racks of lamb (4 ribs each)
2 tablespoons butter

½ cup beef broth

1 cup heavy cream
3 tablespoons capers in brine, drained
1 tablespoon oil with a high smoke point (like peanut, sunflower, corn, vegetable, or safflower oil)
1 teaspoon sea salt

½ teaspoon freshly ground black pepper

Cooking the Rack of Lamb

The sous vide is an ideal method for cooking a rack of lamb, as it allows the meat to be perfectly and evenly cooked throughout. It is best to cook the rack in groups of 4 ribs and then the rack can be quickly seared. For plating, consider slicing the rack into the 4 individual rib portions to show off the color of the meat.

1. Rub the oregano and garlic powder all over the racks of lamb.
2. Fill the water bath with water. Set your sous vide machine temperature to 134°F for medium rare. If a different doneness

for lamb is desired, check *Appendix A: Time and Temperature Charts*.
3. Place the racks of lamb in food-safe bags and vacuum seal the bags. Make sure the racks of lamb are lined up side by side and not stacked or piled. Use multiple bags if necessary.
4. Place the racks of lamb in the water bath and cook sous vide for 4–6 hours.
5. Make the caper cream sauce by melting the butter in a medium saucepan over medium heat. Stir in the beef broth, heavy cream, and capers. Simmer for about 10 minutes, ensuring it doesn't come to a boil.
6. Remove the racks of lamb from the bags and pat dry with a paper towel.
7. Heat the oil in a large skillet over high heat. Sear the racks of lamb in the skillet, meat side down, for about 1–2 minutes. Remove from the skillet and sprinkle with the salt and pepper.
8. To serve, spoon some of the caper cream sauce on each plate. Place a rack of lamb on top of the sauce.

Moroccan Rack of Lamb with Mint Garlic Yogurt Sauce

This Moroccan spice mix, also known as ras el hanout, has a complex taste. The sweet spice is perfect as a rub for the lamb. The yogurt sauce is light and creamy and is a delicate counterbalance to the deep taste in the meat.

Ingredients
Serves 4

1½ teaspoons paprika

1 teaspoon ground cumin

1 teaspoon ground coriander

¼ teaspoon ground cardamom

¼ teaspoon ground cinnamon

¼ teaspoon ground cloves

¼ teaspoon ground nutmeg

1½ teaspoons sea salt, divided

1 teaspoon granulated sugar

4 racks of lamb (4 ribs each)

1 cup plain yogurt

2 tablespoons minced fresh mint

1 clove garlic, minced

1 tablespoon lemon juice

2 tablespoons honey

1 tablespoon oil with a high smoke point (like peanut, sunflower, corn, vegetable, or safflower oil)

½ teaspoon freshly ground black pepper

1. Make the spice rub by mixing together the paprika, cumin, coriander, cardamom, cinnamon, cloves, nutmeg, ½ teaspoon salt, and sugar in small bowl. Rub the spice blend all over the racks of lamb.
2. Fill the water bath with water. Set your sous vide machine temperature to 134°F for medium rare. If a different doneness for lamb is desired, check *Appendix A: Time and Temperature Charts*.
3. Place the racks of lamb in food-safe bags and vacuum seal the bags. Make sure the racks are lined up side by side and not stacked or piled. Use multiple bags if necessary.
4. Place the racks of lamb in the water bath and cook sous vide for 4–6 hours.
5. In a small bowl, mix together the yogurt, mint, minced garlic, lemon juice, and honey. Cover with plastic wrap and place in the fridge until serving time.
6. Remove the racks of lamb from the bag and pat dry with a paper towel.
7. Heat the oil in a large skillet over high heat. Sear the racks of lamb in the skillet, meat side down, for about 1–2 minutes. Remove from the skillet and sprinkle with the remaining salt and the pepper.
8. To serve, place a rack of lamb on each plate and spoon some of the chilled mint garlic yogurt sauce next to it.

Venison Steak with Chipotle Lime Compound Butter

Venison has a deep, rich taste and is an ideal meat cooked sous vide. This compound butter has Southwest flavors that complement the venison nicely.

Ingredients
Serves 4

4 (6-ounce) boneless venison steaks, 1" thick

½ cup salted butter, softened

3 tablespoons minced canned chipotle peppers in adobo sauce

1 tablespoon minced fresh flat-leaf parsley

2 teaspoons lime juice

1 tablespoon oil with a high smoke point (like peanut, sunflower, corn, vegetable, or safflower oil)

1 teaspoon sea salt

½ teaspoon freshly ground black pepper

What about Venison Loin?

If you have a venison loin, the sous vide is a wonderful way to cook this rich meat. It is best to cut the loin into smaller portion-sized pieces. Also note that the cook time for venison is longer than a beef steak since it tends to take longer to tenderize.

---

1. Fill the water bath with water. Set your sous vide machine temperature to 134°F for medium rare. If a different doneness

for venison is desired, check *Appendix A: Time and Temperature Charts*.
2. Place the venison steaks in a food-safe bag and vacuum seal the bag. Make sure the steaks are lined up side by side and not stacked or piled. Use multiple bags if necessary.
3. Place the steaks in the water bath and cook sous vide for about 6–8 hours.
4. Make the compound butter by mixing together the softened butter, minced chipotle peppers, fresh parsley, and lime juice in a medium bowl. Form the butter into a long cylinder that is about 1½" in diameter.
5. Roll up the butter in plastic wrap and twist the ends. Place in the fridge to allow the butter to harden.
6. Remove the venison steaks from the bag and pat dry with a paper towel.
7. Heat the oil in a large skillet over high heat. Sear the steaks in the skillet for about 1–2 minutes per side.
8. Remove the steaks from the skillet and sprinkle with the salt and pepper.
9. Take the compound butter out of the fridge and remove the plastic wrap. Slice the butter into ¼–1/2" rounds.
10. To serve, put a venison steak on each dinner plate and top with 2–3 slices of the compound butter.

Oxtails on Roasted Garlic Potato Mash

The long cook time in this recipe results in meat that is rich in flavor and falls right off the bone. It is best served on a bed of mashed potatoes to ensure that none of that amazing sauce is lost.

Ingredients
Serves 2–3

2 tablespoons vegetable oil

2 pounds oxtails, chopped into 1½" chunks

2 tablespoons tomato paste

3 tablespoons beef broth

1 tablespoon soy sauce

½ teaspoon sea salt

½ teaspoon ground black pepper

5–6 cloves garlic

1 tablespoon olive oil

2 pounds medium potatoes (white, Yukon Gold, or other), peeled and cut into chunks (If desired, make the *Mashed Potatoes* found in Chapter 13)

1 tablespoon butter

¼ cup heavy cream

1. Heat the oil in a large skillet over medium-high heat. Sear the oxtails for about 1 minute per side. Turn the oxtails until all sides have been seared. Remove the oxtails from the skillet and chill.

2. In a medium bowl, whisk together the tomato paste, beef broth, soy sauce, salt, and pepper. Pour over the oxtails and toss until evenly coated.
3. Place the oxtails and sauce in a food-safe bag and vacuum seal the bag. Make sure the oxtails are lined up side by side and not stacked or piled. Use multiple bags if necessary.
4. Fill the water bath with water. Set your sous vide machine temperature to 180°F.
5. Place the oxtails in the water bath and cook sous vide for 18–245 hours.
6. About 1–2 hours before the oxtails are done cooking, preheat the oven to 375°F. Place the garlic in some aluminum foil and drizzle in the olive oil. Wrap up and seal the foil around the garlic. Place the foil package of garlic in the oven and roast for 50–60 minutes.
7. Boil the potatoes until tender. Drain. Make the mashed potatoes by beating together the cooked potatoes, roasted garlic, butter, and heavy cream in a large bowl until smooth.
8. Remove the oxtails from the water bath.
9. To plate, spoon some roasted garlic potato mash on each dinner plate. Place 1 or 2 oxtails on the potato mash and spoon a little sauce from the bag on top of the oxtails.

Alligator Po-Boy Sandwiches with Cajun Mayo

Typically known for being very tough, alligator cooked in the sous vide comes out tender and juicy. These po-boy sandwiches will make you feel like you are in Louisiana.

Ingredients
Serves 4

- 1½ pounds boneless alligator meat (chunks or strips of tail meat), no more than 1" thick
- ½ teaspoon sea salt
- ½ teaspoon freshly ground black pepper
- 2 tablespoons butter
- ½ cup mayonnaise
- 1½ teaspoons Cajun spice or creole seasoning
- 1 teaspoon lemon juice
- 1 teaspoon granulated sugar
- 1 tablespoon oil with a high smoke point (like peanut, sunflower, corn, vegetable, or safflower oil)
- 2 medium tomatoes, thinly sliced
- 1 medium red onion, thinly sliced
- 2 cups sliced iceberg lettuce
- 4 sourdough buns, crusty baguettes, or submarine buns, sliced in half lengthwise

1. Fill the water bath with water. Set your sous vide machine temperature to 167°F.
2. Rub the alligator meat all over with the salt and pepper. Place the alligator meat and butter in a food-safe bag and vacuum seal the bag. Make sure the pieces of meat are in a single layer and not stacked or piled. Use multiple bags if necessary.
3. Place the alligator in the water bath and cook sous vide for 4–6 hours.
4. Make the Cajun mayo by whisking together the mayonnaise, Cajun spice, lemon juice, and sugar in a small bowl. Continue to mix until smooth. Cover with plastic wrap and store in the fridge.
5. Remove the alligator from the bag and pat dry with a paper towel.
6. Heat the oil in a large skillet over high heat. Sear the alligator in the skillet for about 1–2 minutes per side. Slice into ½" strips.
7. Assemble the po-boy sandwiches by spreading some Cajun mayo on the buns. Place some alligator slices, tomatoes, onions, and lettuce on the buns and serve.

Chapter 13
Vegetables and Other Sides

Green Bean Almandine

These perfectly cooked green beans have a nice fresh "bite" and are complemented by the lemon zest and the crunch of the almonds.

Ingredients
Serves 4

3–4 cups trimmed fresh green beans
2 tablespoons olive oil
1 tablespoon lemon zest
2 tablespoons lemon juice
1 teaspoon sea salt

½ cup roughly chopped toasted almonds

Make It Zesty

The zest from citrus fruit adds wonderful fresh aromatic flavors to whatever food it is cooked with. Add some orange zest to brighten up salmon, a little lime zest for some shrimp or rice, and lemon zest goes perfectly with vegetables.

1. Fill the water bath with water. Set your sous vide machine temperature to 183°F.
2. Place the green beans, oil, and lemon zest in a food-safe bag and vacuum seal the bag. Make sure the beans are lined up side by side and not stacked or piled. Use multiple bags if necessary.
3. Place the beans in the water bath and cook sous vide for 45–60 minutes.

4. Remove the green beans from the bag and place on a serving plate. Drizzle with lemon juice and sprinkle with salt.
5. Top with chopped almonds and serve.

Green Bean Almandine

Honey Ginger Carrots

Sous vide is the perfect way to cook carrots and they are highlighted by the delicate flavor of ginger and the sweetness of honey.

Ingredients
Serves 4

1 pound whole baby carrots, peeled
2 tablespoons butter
2 tablespoons honey
2 teaspoons grated fresh gingerroot
1 teaspoon sea salt

1. Fill the water bath with water. Set your sous vide machine temperature to 183°F.
2. Place the carrots, butter, honey, and ginger in a food-safe bag and vacuum seal the bag. Make sure the carrots are lined up side by side and not stacked or piled. Use multiple bags if necessary.
3. Place the carrots in the water bath and cook sous vide for 60–90 minutes.
4. Remove the carrots from the bag and place on a serving plate. Sprinkle with sea salt and serve.

Mashed Potatoes

Making mashed potatoes could not be easier in the sous vide water bath. They are creamy, buttery, and the perfect side dish with many of the meat dishes in this cookbook.

Ingredients
Serves 4

- 2 pounds potatoes (white, Yukon Gold, or other), peeled and cut into 1" chunks
- ¼ cup butter
- ¼ cup heavy cream
- ½ cup whole milk
- ½ teaspoon sea salt
- ½ teaspoon freshly ground black pepper

> **No Grill Required**
>
> Have a classic country barbecue supper, all made in the sous vide, with these Mashed Potatoes, *Buttered Corn on the Cob* (see recipe in this chapter) and *Barbecue Pork Ribs* (see Chapter 10).

1. Fill the water bath with water. Set your sous vide machine temperature to 183°F.
2. Place the chopped potatoes and butter in a food-safe bag and vacuum seal the bag. Make sure the potatoes are lined up side by side and not stacked or piled. Use multiple bags if necessary.

3. Place the potatoes in the water bath and cook sous vide for 1½–2 hours.
4. Drain the potatoes in a large bowl. Add the heavy cream, milk, salt, and pepper. Mash the potatoes with a potato masher or a hand blender.

Maple Butternut Squash Purée

This squash purée is a great side dish and also wonderful as a bed for beef short ribs or pork chops. For extra flare, drizzle a little more maple syrup on the purée and top with toasted pecans.

Ingredients
Serves 4

1 medium butternut squash

⅓ cup maple syrup

¼ cup butter

½ teaspoon sea salt

1. Cut the squash into quarters. Scoop out all the seeds from the inner part of the squash and discard. Peel or cut off the outer skin and discard. Slice the squash flesh into 1" chunks.
2. Fill the water bath with water. Set your sous vide machine temperature to 183°F.
3. Place the squash chunks, maple syrup, butter, and salt in a large food-safe bag and vacuum seal the bag. Make sure that the squash is in a single layer and not stacked. Use multiple bags if necessary.
4. Place the bag in the water bath and cook sous vide for 3 hours.
5. Remove the bag from the water bath and let cool slightly. Pour the squash and any liquid into a food processor or blender and purée until smooth.

Leek and Cauliflower Purée

While this may look like mashed potatoes, it tastes much different. This purée is packed with flavor, and it is healthy too.

Ingredients
Serves 4

2 tablespoons butter

⅔ cup sliced leeks

1 medium head cauliflower

⅔ cup heavy cream

½ teaspoon sea salt

1. In a small saucepan, melt the butter over medium heat. Add the leeks and cook until soft, about 5 minutes. Cool to room temperature.
2. Fill the water bath with water. Set your sous vide machine temperature to 183°F.
3. Cut the cauliflower into ½" slices.
4. Place the cauliflower in a large food-safe bag and vacuum seal the bag. Make sure the cauliflower is placed side by side and not stacked. Use multiple bags if necessary.
5. Place the bag in the water bath and cook sous vide for 2–3 hours.
6. Remove the bag from the water bath and let cool slightly. Place the cauliflower, leeks, heavy cream, and salt into a food processor or blender and purée until smooth.

Szechuan Broccoli

Full of Asian flavors, this sauce has the perfect blend of sweet, salty, sour, and spicy. The broccoli goes great with sous vide chicken and rice.

Ingredients
Serves 4

3 cups small broccoli florets
2 tablespoons olive oil
3 cloves garlic, minced
1 teaspoon grated fresh gingerroot
3 tablespoons soy sauce
2 tablespoons rice vinegar
2 tablespoons granulated sugar
2 tablespoons ketchup

½ teaspoon dried red pepper flakes

2 tablespoons toasted sesame seeds

1. Fill the water bath with water. Set your sous vide machine temperature to 183°F.
2. Place the broccoli in a large food-safe bag and vacuum seal the bag. Make sure the broccoli is placed side by side and not stacked. Use multiple bags if necessary.
3. Place the bag in the water bath and cook sous vide for 1 – 1½ hours.
4. Heat the oil in a medium saucepan over medium heat. Add the garlic and ginger and cook for 2–3 minutes. Add the soy sauce, rice vinegar, sugar, ketchup, and red pepper flakes. Let the sauce simmer for 7–9 minutes. It should thicken slightly.

5. Remove the bag from the water bath. Place the broccoli in a medium bowl and toss with the Szechuan sauce and toasted sesame seeds.

Buttered Corn on the Cob

Corn on the cob may be the perennial vegetable side dish for summer meals. This recipe shows how to cook the cobs in the sous vide water bath.

Ingredients
Serves 4

4 cobs of corn, shucked and cleaned
2 tablespoons butter
1 teaspoon sea salt

1. Fill the water bath with water. Set your sous vide machine temperature to 183°F.
2. Place the corn and butter in a food-safe bag and vacuum seal the bag. Make sure the cobs are lined up side by side and not stacked or piled. Use multiple bags if necessary.
3. Place the corn in the water bath and cook sous vide for 1½–3 hours.
4. Remove the corn from the bag. Sprinkle with sea salt and serve.

Ratatouille

This classic country dish from the Provence region of France is most commonly served as a side dish but can also be served as a main course with pasta.

Ingredients
Serves 4

2 tablespoons olive oil
1 medium sweet onion, diced
1 medium green bell pepper, cored and diced
2 cloves garlic, minced

2 cups peeled and cubed eggplant, no larger than ½" pieces

2 cups cubed zucchini, no larger than ½" pieces
2 medium tomatoes, diced
1 teaspoon sea salt
1 teaspoon dried marjoram or tarragon

½ teaspoon freshly ground black pepper

Why So Long?

Most of the vegetable recipes in this book are cooked for a much shorter amount of time than this recipe. Usually, the vegetables are in the water bath just long enough so that they are cooked through. Ratatouille, though, is more like a stew, and a longer cook time softens the vegetables and blends the flavors wonderfully.

---

1. In a medium skillet, heat oil over medium heat. Add the onion, pepper, and garlic. Cook until the onions are transparent and

the peppers are soft, about 5–7 minutes. Cool to room temperature.
2. Fill the water bath with water. Set your sous vide machine temperature to 183°F.
3. In a large bowl, toss together the sautéed onion and pepper with all the remaining ingredients. Dump the mixture into a food-safe bag and vacuum seal the bag. Make sure the ratatouille is an even thickness within the bag, about 1 – 1½" thick. Use multiple bags if necessary.
4. Place the bag in the water bath and cook sous vide for 3 hours.
5. Remove from the water bath and serve hot.

Chickpea and Carrot Moroccan Stew

Also known as tagine, this classic Moroccan dish has a deep blend of flavors and is perfect served alongside chicken, beef, or couscous.

Ingredients
Serves 4

2 tablespoons olive oil
2 medium sweet onions, diced
2 cloves garlic, minced
3 tablespoons tomato paste
2 tablespoons lemon juice
1 teaspoon ground cumin
1 teaspoon ground coriander
1 teaspoon turmeric
1 teaspoon paprika

½ teaspoon ground cinnamon
1 teaspoon sea salt
2 cups cooked or canned chickpeas
2 cups peeled and sliced carrots
2 medium tomatoes, diced
1 (12-ounce) can black sliced olives
3 tablespoons honey

1. In a medium skillet, heat the oil over medium heat. Add the onion and garlic. Cook until the onions are transparent, about 5–7 minutes. Cool to room temperature.
2. In a small bowl, mix together the tomato paste, lemon juice, and all the spices.

3. Fill the water bath with water. Set your sous vide machine temperature to 183°F.
4. In a large bowl, toss together the sautéed onion, tomato paste mixture, and remaining ingredients, except the honey, until evenly coated. Place the mixture in a food-safe bag and vacuum seal the bag. Make sure the mixture is an even thickness within the bag, about 1 – 1½ inches thick. Use multiple bags if necessary.
5. Place the bag in the water bath and cook sous vide for 3 hours.
6. Remove from the water bath and scoop into a serving bowl. Drizzle with honey and serve.

Wild Mushroom and Leek Risotto

Sautéing the mushrooms and leeks adds a welcome caramelized flavor that enhances the whole risotto dish.

Ingredients
Serves 4

- 2 tablespoons butter
- ⅔ cup sliced leeks
- 2 cups sliced wild mushrooms (such as porcini, oyster, or cremini, or an assortment)
- 2 cloves garlic, minced
- ½ teaspoon sea salt
- ½ teaspoon freshly ground black pepper
- ¼ cup dry white wine
- 1 cup Arborio rice
- 3 cups chicken or vegetable broth
- ½ cup grated Parmesan cheese

1. In a medium sauté pan, melt the butter over medium heat. Add the leeks, mushrooms, garlic, salt, pepper, and white wine. Cook until the leeks and mushrooms are soft, about 5–7 minutes. Cool to room temperature.
2. Fill the water bath with water. Set your sous vide machine temperature to 183°F.
3. Place all the ingredients except the Parmesan cheese in a large food-safe bag and vacuum seal the bag. Make sure the

mixture is an even thickness within the bag, about 1–1½" thick. Use multiple bags if necessary.
4. Place the bag in the water bath and cook sous vide for 65–75 minutes. Every 20 minutes or so, take the bag out and mush it around with your hands to mix up the rice. Use a towel to protect your hands, as the bag will be hot.
5. Pour the risotto into a medium serving bowl. Stir in the Parmesan cheese and serve.

Risotto with Parmesan and Peas

Making risotto on the stovetop requires constant attention and regular stirring. Using the sous vide method simplifies this high-maintenance side dish and the results are creamy and delicious.

Ingredients
Serves 4

2 tablespoons butter
1 medium sweet onion, diced
2 cloves garlic, minced

½ teaspoon sea salt

½ teaspoon freshly ground black pepper

¼ cup dry white wine

1 cup frozen peas, thawed
1 cup Arborio rice
3 cups chicken or vegetable broth

½ cup grated Parmesan cheese
2 tablespoons minced fresh flat-leaf parsley

1. In a medium sauté pan, melt the butter over medium heat. Add the onion, garlic, salt, pepper, and white wine. Cook until the onion is transparent, about 5–7 minutes. Cool to room temperature.
2. Fill the water bath with water. Set your sous vide machine temperature to 183°F.
3. Place all the ingredients except the Parmesan cheese and parsley in a large food-safe bag and vacuum seal the bag.

Make sure the mixture is an even thickness within the bag, about 1–1½" inches thick.
4. Place the bag in the water bath and cook sous vide for 65–75 minutes. Every 20 minutes or so, take the bag out and mush it around with your hands to mix up the rice. Use a towel to protect your hands, as the bag will be hot.
5. Pour the risotto into a medium serving bowl. Stir in the Parmesan cheese and fresh parsley.

Chapter 14
Desserts

Apple Crisp

This recipe allows the apples to be soft and sweet, while the oat crumble stays crunchy. Serve with vanilla ice cream and a drizzle of Dulce de Leche (see recipe in this chapter) on top for a super-decadent dessert.

Ingredients
Serves 4

- 2 cups peeled and diced apples (McIntosh, Gala, Golden Delicious, or other)
- 1¼ packed cups light brown sugar, divided
- 1 teaspoon lemon juice
- ½ cup butter, cut into small cubes
- 1 cup rolled oats
- ¾ cup all-purpose flour
- ½ teaspoon ground cinnamon
- ½ teaspoon salt
- Vanilla ice cream (optional)
- Dulce de Leche (optional—see recipe in this chapter)

Switch Up the Fruit!

Cobblers and crisps are very popular and there are many different varieties. This recipe can easily be modified by using a different fruit. Fresh blueberries, peaches, and raspberries all work well as substitutes for the apples.

1. Fill the water bath with water. Set your sous vide machine temperature to 183°F.
2. Place the apples, ¼ cup brown sugar, and lemon juice in a food-safe bag in an even layer and vacuum seal the bag.
3. Place the apple mixture in the water bath and cook sous vide for 45–60 minutes.
4. Preheat the oven to 350°F.
5. In a large bowl, cut the butter into the remaining 1 cup brown sugar, rolled oats, flour, cinnamon, and salt until it is an even consistency. Spread the mixture evenly across a baking sheet. Bake for 12–15 minutes, until golden brown.
6. To serve, spoon some apple mixture on a plate and top with the crumbly oat mixture. If desired, top with a scoop of vanilla ice cream and drizzle with Dulce de Leche.

Dulce de Leche

This sauce, made from caramelized condensed milk, has never been easier to make than using a sous vide water bath.

Ingredients
Makes about 1 cup

1 (14-ounce) can sweetened condensed milk

1. Fill the water bath with water. Set your sous vide machine temperature to 185°F.
2. Pour the condensed milk in a food-safe bag and vacuum seal the bag.
3. Place the bag in the water bath and cook sous vide for 12–14 hours. The condensed milk should become a deep caramel color.
4. Remove the bag from the water bath and let cool slightly. Drizzle on ice cream, apple crisp, or use to sweeten a coffee or latte.
5. Store in the fridge in a sealed container for up to 2–3 weeks.

Spiced Pumpkin Purée

Nothing screams autumn more than pumpkin and cinnamon. Great on its own, this purée can also be used in a pie, muffins, or even baked with marshmallows on top.

Ingredients
Serves 4

1 sugar pumpkin (about 4–5 pounds)

¾ packed cup light brown sugar

1½ teaspoons ground cinnamon

1 teaspoon ground ginger

½ teaspoon ground nutmeg

¼ teaspoon ground cardamom

¼ teaspoon ground cloves

½ teaspoon salt

¼ cup butter

Make Some Pumpkin Pie!

Mix $2^1/4$ cups pumpkin purée with $1^1/4$ cups heavy cream and 3 eggs until smooth. Pour into an unbaked pie shell. Bake in a 400°F oven for 10 minutes, then lower the oven temperature to 350°F and bake for an additional 25 minutes or until the sides have puffed up and the middle has very little wiggle when the pie is gently shaken back and forth.

1. Cut the pumpkin into quarters. Scoop out all the seeds from the inner part of the pumpkin and discard. Peel or cut off the outer skin and discard. Slice the pumpkin flesh into 1" wedges.
2. Fill the water bath with water. Set your sous vide machine temperature to 183°F.
3. Mix together the brown sugar and spices in a small bowl.
4. Place the pumpkin in a large food-safe bag. Sprinkle in the sugar and spice mixture. Cut the butter into ½" cubes and place in the bag. Make sure that the pumpkin is in a single flat layer and not stacked. Vacuum seal the bag.
5. Place the bag in the water bath and cook sous vide for 3 hours.
6. Remove the bag from the water bath. Pour the pumpkin and the liquid from the bag into a medium bowl and purée it using a stand mixer, potato masher, or hand blender.
7. Serve as a side dish or use for pie filling.

Spiced Pumpkin Purée

Peaches with Brandy

The sous vide water bath gently poaches the peaches in a sweet syrup with brandy. They are delicate and an ideal choice for anyone desiring a light dessert.

Ingredients
Serves 4

½ cup water

½ cup granulated sugar

⅓ cup brandy or cognac

4 large peaches, halved and pitted

Vanilla ice cream (optional)

Crème Anglaise (optional—see recipe in this chapter)

1. In a small saucepan, heat the water and sugar over medium heat, stirring often. Once the sugar has dissolved, remove from heat and cool. Stir in the cognac or brandy and set the syrup aside.
2. Fill the water bath with water. Set your sous vide machine temperature to 183°F.
3. Place the peach halves and syrup in a food-safe bag and vacuum seal the bag. Make sure the peaches are in a single flat layer and not stacked.
4. Place the peaches in the water bath and cook sous vide for 30–45 minutes.
5. Remove from the water bath and immediately place in an ice bath to stop the peaches from continuing to cook.

6. Peel off the skin of the peaches and slice just prior to serving.
7. Serve on its own or with Crème Anglaise or vanilla ice cream.

Peaches with Brandy

Strawberries and Grand Marnier

These early summer berries are wonderful infused in the Grand Marnier (orange liqueur).

Ingredients
Serves 4

3 cups sliced strawberries

¼ cup granulated sugar

2 tablespoons Grand Marnier

½ teaspoon orange zest

2 tablespoons torn fresh mint
Vanilla ice cream (optional)
Crème Anglaise (optional—see recipe in this chapter)

1. Fill the water bath with water. Set your sous vide machine temperature to 183°F.
2. Place the strawberries, sugar, Grand Marnier, and orange zest in a food-safe bag and vacuum seal the bag. Make sure the strawberries are in a single flat layer and not stacked.
3. Place the strawberries in the water bath and cook sous vide for 15 minutes.
4. Remove the bag from the water bath and immediately place in an ice bath to stop the strawberries from continuing to cook.
5. Spoon the strawberries and syrup into serving bowls and top with mint. Serve on its own or with Crème Anglaise or vanilla ice cream.

Crème Anglaise

This sweet custardy sauce is creamy, delicious, and wonderful drizzled on fruit, chocolate cake, and so much more.

Ingredients
Makes about 1 cup

4 large egg yolks

½ cup whole milk

1 cup heavy cream

⅓ cup granulated sugar

1 vanilla bean

1. In a large bowl, whisk together the egg yolks, milk, heavy cream, and sugar. Cut the vanilla bean down the middle and scrape out the all the inner seeds. Put the seeds in the bowl and discard the pod. Whisk the seeds into the cream mixture.
2. Fill the water bath with water. Set your sous vide machine temperature to 175°F.
3. Pour the mixture into a food-safe zip-top bag. Slowly lower the bag into the water using the water displacement method; the air will escape from the bag. Continue to lower the bag until it is about 1" from being fully submerged. Once the bag has been lowered, zip it shut with your fingers.
4. Place the bag in the water bath and cook sous vide for 20–25 minutes.
5. Remove the bag from the water bath and let cool slightly.
6. Serve warm or cold. Store in the fridge in a covered container for up to 1 week.

Pears with Port

This sous vide water bath is the ideal way to make this classic dessert. The pears are soft and gently infused in the spiced port.

Ingredients
Serves 4

2 cups port

¼ cup granulated sugar

1 (1") cinnamon stick
1 whole star anise
2 whole cloves
4 pears (Anjou, Bartlett, or other), peeled, halved, and cored

> **Just Like Poaching**
>
> The sous vide cooking method simulates poaching when liquid is added to the bag along with the fruit, vegetables, or even meat. The nice thing about sous vide is that it requires much less liquid to cover the food than traditional poaching, as the bag coats the food in the liquid once the air is removed and it is vacuum sealed.

1. In a small saucepan, heat the port, sugar, cinnamon stick, star anise, and cloves. Bring to a boil and reduce heat, stirring often. Let the sauce simmer for 2–3 minutes. Take the saucepan off the heat and discard the cinnamon stick, star anise, and cloves. Let the sauce come to room temperature.
2. Fill the water bath with water. Set your sous vide machine temperature to 183°F.
3. Place the pear halves and sauce in a food-safe bag and vacuum seal the bag. Make sure that the pears are in a single

flat layer and not stacked.
4. Place the pears in the water bath and cook sous vide for 45 minutes.
5. Remove from the water bath and immediately place in an ice bath to stop the pears from continuing to cook.
6. Cut open the bag and pour the sauce into a saucepan. Simmer on medium heat to reduce and thicken the sauce.
7. To serve, place 2 pear halves on each plate and pour some of the reduced syrup over the pears.

Mango Pistachio Rice Pudding

Rice pudding is an excellent way to use leftover rice and the mango gives this dessert a wonderful fruity flavor.

Ingredients
Serves 4

1⅓ cups whole milk

⅔ cup heavy cream

3 large eggs

½ cup granulated sugar

1 teaspoon vanilla extract

2 cups cooked white rice (long grain or jasmine)

½ cup diced dried mango

½ cup roughly chopped pistachios

Zip-Top Bags

Some vacuum sealers are not very effective working with liquid in the bags. In these situations, use a large food-safe zipper bag and the water displacement method to remove the air from the bag. Simply fill the bag with the ingredients and slowly lower the bag into the water bath until just the seal is above the water. All the air should be drawn out of the bag. Now just seal the bag with your fingers.

---

1. Fill the water bath with water. Set your sous vide machine temperature to 183°F.

2. In a medium bowl, whisk together the milk, cream, eggs, sugar, and vanilla until smooth. Stir in the cooked rice and dried mango.
3. Pour the rice mixture into a food-safe bag and vacuum seal the bag. Make sure the rice mixture is in an even layer in the bag.
4. Place the rice mixture in the water bath and cook sous vide for 40–45 minutes.
5. Spoon into serving bowls and top with the pistachios.
6. Serve warm or, if desired, chill in the fridge before serving.

Rum Raisin and Pecan Rice Pudding

Rum and raisin is a classic combination and works really well with rice pudding. The toasted pecans provide a welcome crunch to this custardy pudding.

Ingredients
Serves 4

1⅓ cups whole milk

⅔ cup heavy cream

3 large eggs

½ cup granulated sugar

1 teaspoon vanilla extract

1 tablespoon rum

2 cups cooked white rice (long grain or jasmine)

½ cup raisins

½ cup roughly chopped toasted pecans

So Many Variations

There are so many possibilities for rice pudding including dried blueberries, cranberries, or apricots. Toasted almonds or other nuts provide a great crunch to the pudding as well. Satisfy the chocoholic's craving by stirring in some chocolate chips once it comes out of the water bath.

---

1. Fill the water bath with water. Set your sous vide machine temperature to 183°F.

2. In a medium bowl, whisk together the milk, cream, eggs, sugar, vanilla, and rum until smooth. Stir in the cooked rice and raisins.
3. Pour the rice mixture into a food-safe bag and vacuum seal the bag. Make sure the rice mixture is in an even layer in the bag.
4. Place the rice mixture in the water bath and cook sous vide for 40–45 minutes.
5. Spoon into serving bowls and top with the toasted pecans.
6. Serve warm or, if desired, chill in the fridge before serving.

Eggnog

This classic holiday drink is so simple to make in the sous vide and it is creamy and delicious!

Ingredients
Makes about 4 cups

6 large egg yolks
2 cups whole milk

⅔ cup heavy cream

½ cup granulated sugar
1 cup brandy, cognac, or rum (optional)
Pinch ground nutmeg or cinnamon (optional)

1. In a medium bowl, whisk together the egg yolks, milk, heavy cream, and sugar until smooth and creamy.
2. Fill the water bath with water. Set your sous vide machine temperature to 160°F.
3. Pour the mixture into a food-safe zip-top bag. Slowly lower the bag into the water using the water displacement method; the air will escape from the bag. Continue to lower the bag until it is about 1" from being fully submerged. Once the bag has been lowered, zip it shut with your fingers.
4. Place the bag in the water bath and cook sous vide for 75 minutes. Shake up the bag a couple of times during the cooking time.
5. Remove the bag from the water bath and chill. Stir in the brandy, cognac, or rum.

6. Pour into serving glasses and, if desired, sprinkle with nutmeg or cinnamon.

Chapter 15
Pickles, Relishes, and Chutneys

Pickled Dilly Beans

Super tangy, these green beans are incredibly addictive and one is almost never enough.

Ingredients
Makes about 5–6 cups

3 cups green beans

1⅓ cups white vinegar

1 cup water

1 teaspoon sea salt

1–2 sprigs fresh dill

3 cloves garlic, roughly chopped

½ teaspoon dried red pepper flakes

Sous Vide for Pickling?

Using a sous vide water bath is a simple way to make quick pickles. The constant temperature of the water allows the vegetables to be gently blanched in the pickling mixture. This results in vegetables that are tangy but still have a crispy snap to them, and they are ready to eat immediately after they are chilled.

---

1. Fill the water bath with water. Set your sous vide machine temperature to 183°F.
2. Cut off both ends of the green beans.
3. Pour the white vinegar and water into a large bowl. Whisk in the salt until dissolved.
4. Place the green beans, fresh dill, garlic, and red pepper flakes in a large food-safe zipper bag. Pour in the vinegar mixture.

Slowly lower the bag into the water using the water displacement method; the air will escape from the bag. Continue to lower the bag until it is about 1" from being fully submerged. Once the bag has been lowered, zip it shut with your fingers.
5. Cook sous vide for 60–75 minutes.
6. After the sous vide cooking session, immediately place the bag in an ice bath to chill it.
7. Store in a covered glass or plastic container in the fridge for up to 2 weeks.

Bread and Butter Pickles

Sweet and sour, these bread and butter pickles are an awesome lunchtime treat and great on deli sandwiches.

Ingredients
Makes about 4–5 cups

1⅓ cups white vinegar

1⅓ cups granulated sugar

1 teaspoon sea salt

¼ teaspoon turmeric

3 cups sliced pickling cucumbers

½ yellow onion, thinly sliced

1 teaspoon mustard seed

½ teaspoon celery seed

1. Fill the water bath with water. Set your sous vide machine temperature to 183°F.
2. Pour the white vinegar into a large bowl. Whisk in the sugar, salt, and turmeric until dissolved.
3. Place the sliced cucumber, sliced onion, mustard seed, and celery seed in a large food-safe food-safe zipper bag. Pour in the vinegar mixture. Slowly lower the bag into the water using the water displacement method; the air will escape from the bag. Continue to lower the bag until it is about 1" from being fully submerged. Once the bag has been lowered, zip it shut with your fingers.

4. Cook sous vide for 60–75 minutes.
5. After the sous vide cooking session, immediately place the bag in an ice bath to chill it.
6. Store in a covered glass or plastic container in the fridge for up to 2 weeks.

Garlic Dill Pickle Spears

Sous vide is one of the quickest ways to make dill pickles and these spears are crisp, tangy, and a welcome addition to any deli plate.

Ingredients
Makes about 12–16 spears

- 3–4 medium pickling cucumbers
- 1⅓ cups white vinegar
- 1 cup water
- 1½ teaspoons sea salt
- 3 cloves garlic, minced
- 1 sprig fresh dill
- ¼ teaspoon dried red pepper flakes

A Base Recipe

This recipe is excellent used as a base for pickling many other types of vegetables. Simply switch the pickling cucumbers with another veggie like cauliflower, pearl onions, beets, radishes, or sweet banana peppers. Depending on the thickness and hardness of the vegetable, the cooking time may vary. For a hint of sweetness, add a couple of tablespoons of granulated sugar to the mixture.

---

1. Fill the water bath with water. Set your sous vide machine temperature to 183°F.
2. Cut each cucumber into 4 spears by cutting them in half lengthwise and then cutting each half in half lengthwise.
3. Pour the white vinegar and water into a large bowl. Whisk in the salt until dissolved.

4. Place the cucumber spears, minced garlic, fresh dill, and red pepper flakes in a large food-safe zipper bag. Pour in the vinegar mixture. Slowly lower the bag into the water using the water displacement method; the air will escape from the bag. Continue to lower the bag until it is about 1" from being fully submerged. Once the bag has been lowered, zip it shut with your fingers.
5. Cook sous vide for 45–60 minutes.
6. After the sous vide cooking session, immediately place the bag in an ice bath to chill it.
7. Store in a covered glass or plastic container in the fridge for up to 2 weeks.

Spicy Pickled Fennel

Fennel has a mild licorice essence that works nicely with this spicy pickle flavor. Top some sous vide salmon with this pickled fennel for a wonderfully unique taste experience.

Ingredients
Makes about 2–3 cups

1 large fennel bulb

1⅓ cups white vinegar

1 cup water
1 teaspoon sea salt

⅓ cup granulated sugar

3 cloves garlic, roughly chopped
2 medium red Thai chilies, sliced

1. Fill the water bath with water. Set your sous vide machine temperature to 183°F.
2. Chop the fennel bulb into quarters, and then cut each quarter into thin slices.
3. Pour the white vinegar and water into a large bowl. Whisk in the salt and sugar until dissolved.
4. Place the sliced fennel, chopped garlic, and chilies in a large food-safe zipper bag. Pour in the vinegar mixture. Slowly lower the bag into the water using the water displacement method; the air will escape from the bag. Continue to lower the bag until it is about 1" from being fully submerged. Once the bag has been lowered, zip it shut with your fingers.
5. Cook sous vide for 45–60 minutes.

6. After the sous vide cooking session, immediately place the bag in an ice bath to chill it.
7. Store in a covered glass or plastic container in the fridge for up to 2 weeks.

Vietnamese Pickled Carrots and Daikon

Brightly colored orange and white with both a sweet and zippy pickled taste, these are commonly served on Vietnamese banh mi sandwiches.

Ingredients
Makes about 4–5 cups

1 large daikon
2 medium or large carrots
1 cup white vinegar

1⅓ cups water

2 teaspoons sea salt

⅓ cup granulated sugar

1. Fill the water bath with water. Set your sous vide machine temperature to 183°F.
2. Peel the daikon and carrots and julienne them. They should be about ¼" wide and 2–3" long.
3. Pour the white vinegar and water into a large bowl. Whisk in the salt and sugar until dissolved.
4. Place the julienned daikon and carrots in a large food-safe zipper bag. Pour in the vinegar mixture. Slowly lower the bag into the water using the water displacement method; the air will escape from the bag. Continue to lower the bag until it is about 1" from being fully submerged. Once the bag has been lowered, zip it shut with your fingers.
5. Cook sous vide for 45–60 minutes.

6. After the sous vide cooking session, immediately place the bag in an ice bath to chill it.
7. Store in a covered glass or plastic container in the fridge for up to 2 weeks. Serve on banh mi sandwiches or eat them straight out of the jar.

Pickled Red Onions

The onions are lightly blanched in the pickling mixture, giving them a sour tang and crispy bite. These are excellent as a topper on burgers, hot dogs, sausages, and pulled pork.

Ingredients
Makes about 3 cups

- 1 large red onion
- 1⅓ cups white vinegar
- 1 cup water
- 1 teaspoon sea salt
- 2 tablespoons granulated sugar
- 1 teaspoon freshly ground black pepper

> **An Ideal Condiment**
>
> One taste of these pickled onions will inspire you with ways to incorporate crisp and sour pickled veggies to a variety of dishes. Serve this with cilantro chimichurri on a sous vide halibut for one amazing taste experience. It is also delicious on sous vide chicken breast with sun-dried tomato pesto. The possibilities are endless.

1. Fill the water bath with water. Set your sous vide machine temperature to 183°F.
2. Peel the red onion and cut it into ¼" slices.
3. Pour the white vinegar and water into a large bowl. Whisk in the salt, sugar, and black pepper until the salt and sugar are dissolved.
4. Place the sliced red onion in a large food-safe zipper bag. Pour in the vinegar mixture. Slowly lower the bag into the water

using the water displacement method; the air will escape from the bag. Continue to lower the bag until it is about 1" from being fully submerged. Once the bag has been lowered, zip it shut with your fingers.
5. Cook sous vide for 45–60 minutes.
6. After the sous vide cooking session, immediately place the bag in an ice bath to chill it.
7. Store in a covered glass or plastic container in the fridge for up to 2 weeks.

Pickled Jalapeño Escabeche

Awesome as a topping for tacos or fajitas, this classic Mexican accompaniment is a snap to make in the sous vide water bath.

Ingredients
Makes about 5 cups

6–8 medium jalapeño peppers
1 large carrot

½ medium red onion

1⅓ cups white vinegar
1 cup water
1 teaspoon sea salt
2 teaspoons granulated sugar

1. Fill the water bath with water. Set your sous vide machine temperature to 183°F.
2. Cut the jalapeño peppers into ¼" slices. Peel the carrot and cut into thin round slices. Peel the onion and slice thinly.
3. Pour the white vinegar and water into a large bowl. Whisk in the salt and sugar until dissolved.
4. Place the sliced jalapeño peppers, carrot, and onion in a large food-safe zipper bag. Pour in the vinegar mixture. Slowly lower the bag into the water using the water displacement method; the air will escape from the bag. Continue to lower the bag until it is about 1" from being fully submerged. Once the bag has been lowered, zip it shut with your fingers.
5. Cook sous vide for 60–75 minutes.

6. After the sous vide cooking session, immediately place the bag in an ice bath to chill it.
7. Store in a covered glass or plastic container in the fridge for up to 2 weeks.

Pickled Turnips

Classic as a topping for shawarmas, these turnips are stained purple from the beet during the pickling process.

Ingredients
Makes about 4–5 cups

3–4 medium turnips
1 medium beet
1 cup white vinegar

1⅓ cups water

2 teaspoons sea salt

⅓ cup granulated sugar

2 cloves garlic, roughly chopped

1. Fill the water bath with water. Set your sous vide machine temperature to 183°F.
2. Peel the turnips and cut them into sticks, similar in shape to french fries. Peel the beet and cut into quarters.
3. Pour the white vinegar and water into a large bowl. Whisk in the salt and sugar until dissolved.
4. Place the turnip sticks, beet quarters, and chopped garlic in a large food-safe zipper bag. Pour in the vinegar mixture. Slowly lower the bag into the water using the water displacement method; the air will escape from the bag. Continue to lower the bag until it is about 1" from being fully submerged. Once the bag has been lowered, zip it shut with your fingers.
5. Cook sous vide for 45–60 minutes.

6. After the sous vide cooking session, immediately place the bag in an ice bath to chill it.
7. Store in a covered glass or plastic container in the fridge for up to 2 weeks. Serve on *Chicken Shawarmas* (see Chapter 8) or eat them straight out of the jar.

Zucchini Relish

Making relish in a sous vide water bath is very easy and the results are impressive. This relish is a nice twist from standard cucumber relish and is great served on hot dogs, sausages, burgers, and more.

Ingredients
Makes about 4–5 cups

1 cup white vinegar
1 cup granulated sugar
1 teaspoon sea salt
3 cups grated zucchini
1 medium red bell pepper, cored and diced

½ sweet onion, minced

1. Fill the water bath with water. Set your sous vide machine temperature to 183°F.
2. Pour the white vinegar into a large bowl. Whisk in the sugar and salt until dissolved.
3. Place the grated zucchini, red pepper, and onion in a large food-safe zipper bag. Pour in the vinegar mixture. Slowly lower the bag into the water using the water displacement method; the air will escape from the bag. Continue to lower the bag until it is about 1" from being fully submerged. Once the bag has been lowered, zip it shut with your fingers.
4. Cook sous vide for 75–90 minutes.
5. After the sous vide cooking session, immediately place the bag in an ice bath to chill it.

6. Store in a covered glass or plastic container in the fridge for up to 2 weeks.

Sweet Cucumber Relish

This sweet relish is far superior to anything you could purchase at a supermarket and is perfect for any backyard barbecue. Top a hot dog with some of this relish, a few Pickled Red Onions (see recipe in this chapter), and a squirt of mustard.

Ingredients
Makes about 4–5 cups

1 cup white vinegar
1 cup granulated sugar
1 teaspoon sea salt
1 teaspoon mustard seed

½ teaspoon celery seed

¼ teaspoon turmeric

3 cups finely peeled and diced cucumber
1 medium yellow bell pepper, cored and diced

½ yellow onion, minced

1. Fill the water bath with water. Set your sous vide machine temperature to 183°F.
2. Pour the white vinegar into a large bowl. Whisk in the sugar, salt, mustard seed, celery seed, and turmeric until the sugar and salt are dissolved.
3. Place the diced cucumber, yellow pepper, and onion in a large food-safe zipper bag. Pour in the vinegar mixture. Slowly lower the bag into the water using the water displacement method; the air will escape from the bag. Continue to lower the bag until

it is about 1" from being fully submerged. Once the bag has been lowered, zip it shut with your fingers.
4. Cook sous vide for 75–90 minutes.
5. After the sous vide cooking session, immediately place the bag in an ice bath to chill it.
6. Store in a covered glass or plastic container in the fridge for up to 2 weeks.

Tomato Pineapple Chutney

This simple chutney is an ideal topping for many different meats like steak, pork chops, chicken, and more.

Ingredients
Makes about 4 cups

⅓ cup white vinegar

½ cup granulated sugar

1 teaspoon sea salt

½ teaspoon garlic powder

1½ cups finely diced tomatoes

1½ cups finely diced pineapple

1 medium red bell pepper, cored and diced

½ red onion, minced

⅓ cup minced fresh cilantro

1. Fill the water bath with water. Set your sous vide machine temperature to 183°F.
2. Pour the white vinegar into a large bowl. Whisk in the sugar, salt, and garlic powder until dissolved.
3. Place the diced tomatoes, pineapple, red pepper, red onion, and cilantro in a large food-safe zipper bag. Pour in the vinegar mixture. Slowly lower the bag into the water using the water displacement method; the air will escape from the bag. Continue to lower the bag until it is about 1" from being fully

submerged. Once the bag has been lowered, zip it shut with your fingers.
4. Cook sous vide for 75–90 minutes.
5. After the sous vide cooking session, immediately place the bag in an ice bath to chill it.
6. Store in a covered glass or plastic container in the fridge for up to 2 weeks.

Peach and Mango Chutney

Bright and fruity with a little spice, this chutney is delicious all on its own, but excellent served on fish or chicken.

Ingredients
Makes about 4 cups

⅓ cup white vinegar

½ cup granulated sugar

1 teaspoon sea salt

½ teaspoon ground cumin

½ teaspoon ground cinnamon

¼ teaspoon ground ginger

1½ cups pitted and finely diced peaches

1½ cups pitted and finely diced mangos

1 medium red bell pepper, cored and diced

2 medium jalapeño peppers, cored and diced

½ red onion, minced

⅓ cup minced fresh cilantro

Variations

There are so many different options and possibilities with this chutney recipe. You can change up the fruit with others like apricots, pears, or apples. Also, try adding some dried fruit like raisins, dried cranberries, or dried cherries to the recipe.

1. Fill the water bath with water. Set your sous vide machine temperature to 183°F.
2. Pour the white vinegar into a large bowl. Whisk in the sugar, salt, cumin, cinnamon, and ginger until dissolved.
3. Place the diced peaches, mangos, red pepper, jalapeño peppers, red onion, and cilantro in a large food-safe zipper bag. Pour in the vinegar mixture. Slowly lower the bag into the water using the water displacement method; the air will escape from the bag. Continue to lower the bag until it is about 1" from being fully submerged. Once the bag has been lowered, zip it shut with your fingers.
4. Cook sous vide for 75–90 minutes.
5. After the sous vide cooking session, immediately place the bag in an ice bath to chill it.
6. Store in a covered glass or plastic container in the fridge for up to 2 weeks.

Printed in Great Britain
by Amazon